# Table of Contents

Abstract ..................................................

Contributors ..........................................

Introduction ..........................................

Chapter 1: Practising Commercial Law as a Career .................................................. 8

Chapter 2: Employability and Careers ................................................................... 19

Chapter 3: Working in Different Departments ........................................................ 31

Chapter 4: Making decisions as a Newly Qualified Solicitor ................................... 67

Chapter 5: Working In-House .................................................................................. 80

Chapter 6: Understanding Diversity & Inclusion in the Legal Sector ..................... 104

Chapter 7: Advice for Aspiring Lawyers ................................................................. 120

Conclusion .............................................................................................................. 135

# Abstract

The purpose of this project is to provide a collection of unfiltered insights from paralegals, trainee solicitors, associates and partners working across the legal sector at a range of organisations including in-house companies and private practice law firms.

This resource will be beneficial to aspiring lawyers trying to break into the profession but also trainee solicitors looking to move onto the next seat and final seat trainee solicitors looking to gain insight on how to prepare for qualification.

This book focuses on topics such as Mental Health and Diversity and Inclusion by featuring legal professionals from BAME and LGBT+ backgrounds.

All contributors gave consent to their responses being included in the book. Each contributor was also asked to consent for their name and employment title to be included in the book.

All royalties and proceeds raised for this book will be used to create a scholarship fund to support students wishing to pursue the GDL and/or LPC.

# Contributors

Adam Hattersley
Associate
Fieldfisher

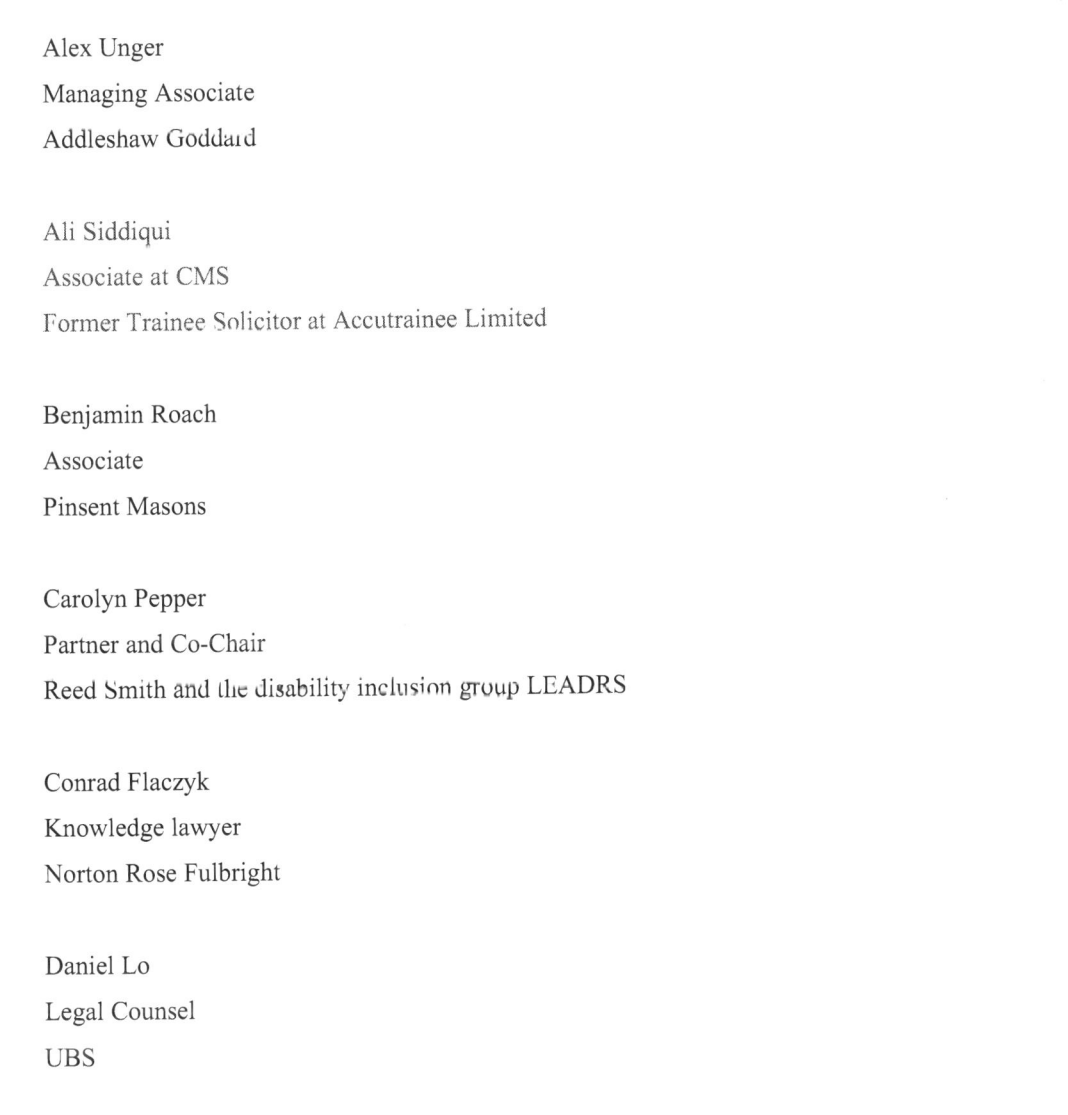

Amelia Wilson
Trainee Solicitor
Channel 4

Alex Unger
Managing Associate
Addleshaw Goddard

Ali Siddiqui
Associate at CMS
Former Trainee Solicitor at Accutrainee Limited

Benjamin Roach
Associate
Pinsent Masons

Carolyn Pepper
Partner and Co-Chair
Reed Smith and the disability inclusion group LEADRS

Conrad Flaczyk
Knowledge lawyer
Norton Rose Fulbright

Daniel Lo
Legal Counsel
UBS

Daniel Harris
Associate Director
Robert Walters Legal Recruitment Company

Deepti Patankar
Founder of Hostmaker.co
Ex-Associate at Linklaters

Donya Fredj
Corporate Lawyer

Jade Naylor
Trainee Solicitor
Pinsent Masons

Jahed Hussain
Legal Counsel
Euro Car Parts Limited

Jason Feng
Construction Lawyer
Pinsent Masons

Jennifer O'Kane
Trainee Solicitor
Simmons & Simmons

Joanna Middlemass
Paralegal and Future Trainee Solicitor
Addleshaw Goddard and Ashurst

John Watkins
Director of Employability
University of Law

Laura Durrant
Director of Howlett Brown Limited

Louise Formisano
Trainee Solicitor
CMS

Lukas Vician
Trainee Solicitor
CMS

Matthew Wilson
Associate General Counsel, EMEA & APAC
Uber

Melissa Kinsmore-Ward
Associate
Akin Gump Strauss Hauer & Feld

Niall McCluskey
Advocate
Optimum Advocates, Glasgow

Robert Hanna
Founder
Kissoon Carr

Sajeed Jamal
Trainee Solicitor
Trowers & Hamlins

Sakhee Gantra
Associate
Mishcon de Reya

Scott Halliday
Associate
Irwin Mitchell

Simon Colvin
Global Head of Technology
Pinsent Masons

Sofia Aslam
Trainee Solicitor
Ashurst

Umar Jamil
Paralegal and Future Trainee Solicitor
Hogan Lovells and Macfarlanes

Vaibhav Adlakha
Associate
Reed Smith

Vikash Vaitha
Lead Paralegal
Pinsent Masons

Special thanks to Dave Kerpen, Lauren Moore, Sana Shafi, Simra Khadam and Mohima Khan who supported the delivery of this book.

# Introduction

I recently secured a training contract with Pinsent Masons after graduating from a degree in International Relations. The objective of this book emerged from my curiosity with the legal sector and the realisation that there was so much I did not yet know about the career I was pursuing.

There are no two ways about it - a career in commercial law is tough to break into. With a finite amount of training contracts available for a large pool of talented and intelligent candidates, it is important to understand the career you are applying for.

The objective of this book is to connect legal professionals at different stages in their careers to you, the reader. Each professional will share their insight, having made career moves that you might or might not have experienced or considered.

This book is not exclusive to aspiring solicitors. I have tried to break down each phase of legal journeys. This book might interest you if you are:

i. An aspiring solicitor interested in learning more about the legal sector.
ii. A paralegal who wants to learn from other paralegals that recently obtained training contracts.
iii. A trainee solicitor moving into a different department and want to hear from another trainee solicitor who has recently completed that seat.
iv. A final seat trainee solicitor preparing for qualification.
v. Looking to move in-house.
vi. Interested in commercial law.

As a heads up, this book is aimed to be free flowing and as unfiltered as possible. Certain parts will have a more relaxed tone (which I hope you enjoy). Feel free to flick through to the parts that interest you most!

# Chapter 1: Practising Commercial Law as a Career

This chapter aims to introduce what a career in commercial law involves. The majority of aspiring solicitors have an idea however, this section aims to demystify a career in commercial law. This has been achieved by sharing the experiences of a variety of legal professionals. With the strong focus that is placed on securing a training contract, I also wanted to share insight from legal professionals who pursued alternative routes into the industry to become a solicitor.

**What is a commercial lawyer:**

To kick things off, I draw upon what a commercial lawyer actually means. During university, the majority of students experience the milk round of commercial law firms presenting great opportunities with this path perhaps being imprinted as the primary goal. However, is this for you? Whilst there might be an idealised notion of what a career in commercial law means - I thought it would be important to break down the reality. A career in commercial law is a great path but it is not for everyone. Thus, it is beneficial to have all the facts in front of you before deciding. Alex Unger who is the Managing Associate at Addleshaw Goddard shares below his career experiences and reflects on life working as a lawyer in London:

"Working as an associate at a City firm offers an unparalleled insight into the world of business. The City is a global financial powerhouse, and the law firms that operate in it work with some of the world's biggest clients on their biggest deals and cases. In that respect it is a huge learning curve-the pace, complexity and sheer size of some of the matters you work on all mean that you have to learn very quickly, be adaptable, hardworking and to have a desire to continually improve. With all of that comes the opportunity to learn from some of the best lawyers in the UK, and to work right at the cutting edge of the global legal market.

Aside from that, the City (at least before COVID-19) is a great place to work, with interesting people from a huge variety of backgrounds, and plenty of socialising. In day to day terms, it really varies depending on the department you are in. As a litigation associate there is hardly ever a 'typical' day, but my day will invariably include lots of reading, drafting correspondence to the other side, preparing notes of advice to my clients, planning case strategy and preparing court documents. There is always plenty to do."

Jason Feng, a Construction lawyer at Pinsent Masons based in Australia, adds his perspective of what a career in commercial law means in practice: "I think the biggest misconception I had was that lawyers were predominately concerned with creating a technically perfect legal product. While that is important, it is only one (important) part of the job. Now I have learned that the modern lawyer wears many different hats - project manager, salesman, mentor as well as being somebody that understands technology and financials.

While this might seem intimidating, it actually means that there are multiple ways for us as young lawyers to play to our unique strengths and excel. Being the technically perfect savant is only one of the ways to achieve success in this industry."

## **The difference between a Barrister and a Solicitor:**

The starting point for me, which I imagine many other aspiring lawyers consider, was to decide to pursue the barrister or solicitor route. But how do you know what the difference is? Matthew Wilson, Associate General Counsel for EMEA & APAC at Uber, breaks down the jargon explaining:

"In terms of being a solicitor, there are the technical differences and then there are the practical differences. For me, the technical difference between a solicitor and a barrister are generally that solicitors advise more broadly across a range of different subject areas whereas barristers tend to be a bit more specialised. However, you do get barristers that are specialists in a variety of different areas. Historically the technical difference has been the 'rights of audience'. The ability to stand up in a courtroom and advocate on behalf of your client has historically rested with barristers. There is now a category called solicitor advocates now who are solicitors that do extra qualifications to be admitted in order to have the ability to similar rights of audience too.

I often think of barristers as hired guns. Barristers have unique skills to dig into very specific elements of the law, predict how courts are likely to view novel situations and to cogently, coherently and persuasively advance an argument using their sharp legal minds, barristers often bring a different and alternative clarity of thought to strategic conversations and litigation strategy. You then have the criminal bar which is another thing entirely as you are often representing individuals instead of companies. The barrister would either act for the prosecution or the defence.

From a solicitor point of view, the job can be very broad. In some ways what you are doing as a solicitor is giving advice based combining your knowledge and experience of how the world works and what the law is. It is like a business consultancy in some respects but with a legal lens. If you move in-house you become that of a commercial business partner. Your role is not just to advise on the law, but to work out sustainable solutions using that knowledge. I probably spend about 30% of my time dispensing direct legal advice and 70% of my time spent on giving business advice based on my legal training and my experience at firms and commercial law.

With solicitors, there is such a wide variety of career paths and choices. You have everything from, for example, family law to private equity. Those two areas of specialism could not be more different."

**Becoming a lawyer in Scotland:**

This book shares insight into individuals becoming lawyers based in the UK and beyond. I thought it would be important to specifically understand how the process works in Scotland. This is achieved by sharing the insight of Niall McCluskey who is an Advocate at Optimum Advocates based in Glasgow:

"An Advocate is an independent legal professional and member of the Faculty of Advocates the professional body they are regulated by. Advocates are very similar to barristers in England. Advocates have rights of audience in the highest courts such as the High Court of Justiciary (Criminal), the Court of Session (Civil) and Supreme Court. Advocates are always self-employed and cannot form partnerships.

Solicitors have a direct connection with clients. The clients that advocates represent are in fact solicitor's clients because solicitor's instruct advocates in certain cases and that is how we get our work. Solicitors are akin to GPs and advocates to consultants. Only in exceptional defined circumstances can advocates take direct instructions but the bulk of instructions come from solicitors. All my work comes from solicitors.

Solicitors do not have rights of audience in the highest courts such as the High Court of Justiciary (Criminal), the Court of Session (Civil) and Supreme Court but do appear regularly in courts such as the Sheriff Court.

Solicitors are regulated by the Law Society of Scotland and are allowed to form partnerships. Solicitor advocates are solicitors who also have rights of audience in the highest courts such as the High Court of Justiciary (Criminal), the Court of Session (Civil) and Supreme Court and also appear regularly in courts such as the Sheriff Court. They effectively have a hybrid qualification however strict boundaries apply. If they are acting in a case akin to an advocate, they cannot also be the solicitor, although someone else in their firm can act as solicitor and instruct them. Vice versa when acting as solicitor they cannot also act in the case in the advocate role.

I work primarily as a Criminal Defence Counsel which means I conduct trials in the High Court. The types of crime that commonly come up are Murder, Attempted Murder, Culpable Homicide, Rape, Sexual offences, Drugs cases and Death by Dangerous Driving. I also conduct jury trials in the Sheriff Court. In addition, I appear in Criminal appeals.

I have also acted in Extradition and Immigration cases and appeared in a number of tribunals such as the Employment tribunal and the Mental Health tribunal. I have also acted in Professional Disciplinary cases.

**Career highlights:**

Regularly winning Criminal trials across a broad range of types of allegations. I was very pleased in a recent case where I represented a young man in the High Court facing a very serious allegation and he was found unanimously not guilty of a very serious charge. Had he been convicted he would have gone to prison and even when he came out his life would have been ruined.

Winning extradition cases and helping individuals remain in the UK. I am particular proud of blocking an extradition request to the United Arab Emirates on behalf of a client. This was particularly important because the UAE has an appalling human rights record.

Winning Immigration cases where individuals were allowed to stay in the UK. This has helped them to live a better life.

**What makes a successful Advocate in Scotland:**

i. Very hard work preparing your cases with a strong attention to detail.
ii. Being committed to doing your best to represent your client and to being an officer of the court.
iii. Keeping up to date which changes in law and procedure.
iv. Being creative and strategic in how you approach your cases.
v. Developing your advocacy skills so you perform at your best in court.
vi. Being able to get on well with solicitors who instruct you, network well with solicitors you want to instruct you and have good interpersonal skills with clients."

**Alternative routes into the legal sector:**

Outside of securing a training contract there are a number of different paths you can take to enter the profession. In the United Kingdom, the Solicitors Regulation Authorities decided to introduce The Solicitors Qualifying Exam. This is an alternative route to qualifying as a lawyer in England and Wales. This decision creates greater accessibility to the profession by enabling aspiring solicitors to become lawyers outside of the traditional training contract route. This traditional model is spent over two years with one firm and the new model can instead be spread across different organisations.

Another route is the Chartered Institute of Legal Executives also known as CILEx. With thousands of CILEx professionals in the sector they play an important role to supporting the activities of law firms. CILEx are made up of paralegals and other practitioners working in the legal sector. CILEx professionals are involved in a range of legal areas including: litigation, conveyancing, personal injury as well as probate cases involving trusts. The Solicitors Regulation Authority can recognise this in pursuit of becoming a qualified solicitor, but this should be further discussed directly with their team as there are a number of factors that can affect your eligibility.

For many aspiring solicitors this is a desirable option. Working as a paralegal is another option to build up your experience and rapport with law firms in pursuit of a training contract. Maybe for some but not for all, at this point, you might be wondering what a paralegal is and what they do? A paralegal provides legal assistance and are trained to assist solicitors with a number of roles and responsibilities.

A key difference between the roles is that trainee solicitors often rotate departments ('seats') every six months, whereas paralegals remain within a specific department. As a result, paralegals often gain more experience in one practice area. However, by the same token trainee solicitors are exposed to more practice areas and gain a greater insight into other departments within the firm.

To shed more light on this, I turn to paralegals who are either currently working in the role or recently secured training contracts off the back of working as a paralegal. First up is Umar Jamil who was a paralegal at Hogan Lovells and is now a future trainee solicitor at Macfarlanes. Umar shares his experience explaining:

"I come from a non-traditional background, being state school educated, from a BAME background and being the first in my family to have attended university. As an undergraduate I studied law, because I enjoyed Economics and Law at A-level, in particular the commercial mindset required in Economics and the critical thinking aspect of Law.

After graduating from the University of Birmingham in 2018, I commenced the LLM LPC on a part-time basis, whilst also building my practical skills through paralegal placements at international law firms. After a year of working as a paralegal and studying the LPC, I began applying for vacation schemes and training contracts, and I secured a vacation scheme offer at an international firm as well as a training contract offer at Macfarlanes, of which I accepted the latter.

At Hogan Lovells, I worked as a paralegal in the Legal Services Centre at the firm's Birmingham office. My role predominantly involved supporting the London office, particularly the commercial litigation team on the disclosure stage of litigation projects. This included operating legal technology products such as an artificial intelligence-based e-discovery platform to review complex documents and decide on their relevance to the litigation. Not only did this experience develop my communication and analytical skills, but it also gave me an understanding of how technology can be utilised to reduce costs and speed up processes for a client.

The reason why I chose the paralegal route instead of pursuing a training contract after graduating was because I was undecided on a career in law. Therefore, I explored other career options (i.e. banking and accountancy) and attended insight events at various law firms, which led to me firmly deciding to pursue a legal career.

Naturally, the next steps for me were to continue building my skills through embarking on the LPC whilst undertaking paralegal work. This route was attractive because I lacked the understanding of what the work of a lawyer involved, and through the LPC I was able to pick up vital skills such as legal writing which I was able to put into practice when working as a paralegal. Significantly, my paralegal experience helped instil in me the confidence that I could succeed in a legal career, which I was then able to transfer to my applications and demonstrate at assessment days."

The next contributor we turn to is Joanna Middlemass who recently secured a training contract at Ashurst after being a paralegal at Addleshaw Goddard for two years:

"I studied Law LLB at the University of York, graduating in July 2018. I joined Addleshaw Goddard in the same month and gained a training contract at Ashurst in November 2018. I have worked in real estate at Addleshaw Goddard for the last two years. In my opinion, a career in commercial law means constantly being challenged. It means balancing commercial objective and the law, where market conditions are continuously changing. This is what drew me to a career in law; I wanted a career where I would never stop learning.

My daily responsibilities as a paralegal at Addleshaw Goddard varied. I was 'embedded' on a single client team. This means I generally only did work for them. I managed approximately thirty matters with supervision. I was responsible for these matters from their inception, drafting and negotiation to completion, post-completion and billing.

I had significant client contact, which means I was in contact with the client throughout the day. I was responsible for reporting to the client and cascading key messages down to the rest of the client team.

As the embedded paralegal, I was also responsible for identifying opportunities for efficiency creation. I worked closely with the Innovation and Legal Technology (ILT) Team to test and implement solutions for the client. These have included, streamlining internal processes and the allocation of resource within the client team, and automating the client's precedent documents.

Aside from my client work, I sometimes did ad hoc work or project management as required by the business. For example, I was heavily involved in coordinating the completion of several hundred certificates of title. I had been a paralegal at Addleshaw Goddard on a fixed-term three-month contract during my second year at university.

In my mind, committing myself to three months of employment showed an unquestionable commitment to a career in law. It exposes you to the pressures and stresses of a corporate environment. You have deadlines, you will deal with unavailable and uncooperative clients. This is what makes the experience so valuable. It enabled me to say unequivocally 'I know I want to do this because I am doing it'.

Further, choosing firms you want to apply to is a minefield. Working in a firm enables you to identify what you value in a firm and what you do not. Working at Addleshaw Goddard enabled me to draw a comparison with Ashurst and substantiate why I wanted a training contract. This is really important in answering 'motivational' questions and setting yourself apart as a candidate that has done their research.

I have recently been involved in various projects as a result of COVID-19. These projects, generally, tried to mitigate the commercial impacts of the Government's measures on Tenants and Landlords. My role was to collate information that was essential to the wider transaction and feed it to fee-earners within Addleshaw Goddard and the other firms we were working with. We worked tirelessly towards strict commercial deadlines. However, because the laws enacted in response to the global pandemic and were unprecedented, we did not know what the outcome of our work would be.

At the beginning of my time at Addleshaw Goddard, I also played a coordinating role in one of the largest project real estate had been involved in since the recession. I was responsible for commissioning searches and processing the results. The sheer volume of work often meant that I had to deal with competing commercial priorities. I have found the most valuable priority, commercially, to be time!

The most transferable skills I have developed as a paralegal are interpersonal skills. A lot of the work of a paralegal requires you to work in a small, close-knit team or directly with an individual fee-earner. As a consequence, a key skill is people management. Everyone I have worked with has had a preferred way to instruct, supervise and/or provide feedback. Some fee-earners want to be continually updated and other's just want to know when their instruction has been completed.

This requires you to adjust the way you approach that fee-earner and communicate with them. The same applies to clients. This means I am well-practiced in communicating with a diverse range of people and expressing myself clearly. This is an advantage in a training contract interview and will be an advantage as a trainee solicitor. Further, my interaction with my colleagues and clients made me feel more confident going into the interview."

Finally, we move onto the last contribution from Vikash Vaitha, who has been a paralegal for several years in an effort to develop his skills and secure a training contract. For the last two years Vikash has elevated to lead paralegal in the Corporate team at Pinsent Masons. Here are his tips on how to advance your chances of securing a training contract by choosing the paralegal route:

"I have always wanted a career in law and really became fascinated with commercial law after learning about the financial crisis in 2007/2008. I particularly enjoyed learning how geopolitical tensions, sectors and society at large became affected by the turmoil caused in a concentrated area of finance.

A career in commercial law is interesting to me because of the varied nature of the work and clients. For example, clients in the energy sector will have particular objectives or commercial considerations, be affected by current markets, which we need to quickly adapt to and understand. Similarly, working with financial institutions has its own challenges, interesting topics and regulations which need to be considered before and during transactions. Nuances like this and the learning opportunities are what keep me energised in working for a commercial law firm. Everything is relevant.

I read a few economics books which helped better my understanding of financial markets and how businesses make decisions. Books such as 'Misbehaving' and 'Nudge' by Richard Thaler explored behavioural economics and examined the flaws in economic policy by not considering human behaviour. Furthermore, 'Principles' by Ray Dalio and 'What it Takes' by Stephen Schwarzman gave me great insight into managing my own brand and how to make the most of learning opportunities. This has enhanced my understanding of commercial law as I was able to apply the principles from experts into my everyday role in a law firm.

At Pinsent Masons, I work for a team called the Transactional Services Paralegal Hub. We are a team of paralegals who serve the corporate, commercial, employment and competition practices of Pinsent Masons. My role as a lead paralegal is to maintain a sufficient workflow from the national corporate and commercial teams (sometimes dipping into finance and TMT).

I present in team meetings, pitch to clients and sell an efficient service by assigning project work to paralegals based on their ability, experience and general interest. As a manager, I am responsible for maintaining a quality and efficient output and gaining new opportunities for my team to experience meaningful work. So far, my team has assisted on project management for transactions, assisted with verification for corporate finance projects and carried out commercial contract reviews for transition agreements.

Why did I choose to become a paralegal? Honestly, to pay bills. Getting a training contract is proving to be one of the most difficult and competitive tasks I have ever undertaken, and I needed to start paying LPC loans pretty soon after finishing. Thankfully, Pinsent Masons gave me an opportunity and I have developed a greater understanding of the legal industry and various practice areas since joining. If anyone is unsure about entering the legal industry, I would definitely encourage applicants to explore a paralegal role to gain a real feel of what legal work entails.

I have found some practice areas more exciting than others, similarly with sectors, all which have shaped my thinking and work ethic today. Having worked on many transactions, I would consider work in corporate finance to be exciting due to its market impact and real-time application. For example, a client in the middle of the pandemic began to worry about the effects of the pandemic on their business. We needed to re-evaluate the situation day-by-day and propose new strategies for pushing our client's objectives. We analysed competitor strategies and quickly adapted our understanding to what the market told us about this particular sector.

In the end, our project, which started as a typical M&A transaction transformed into a corporate finance transaction, which took place over a weekend due to the unpredictable and uncertain nature of the coronavirus on businesses. The client was extremely pleased with our quick turnaround and commitment to pushing through their objectives. This was rewarding for me personally as I gained significant responsibility during the transition phases."

At this point you might be thinking - this has focused on the early stages of entering the legal profession. What does a career in commercial law actually involve next?

Chapter 2 aims to break down a career further and the following chapter looks at the life of a trainee solicitor working in different departments at a law firm. This might be beneficial for aspiring solicitors looking to understand more about the industry they seek to enter.

Additionally, this might be beneficial for existing trainee solicitors who wish to learn more about an upcoming seat, particularly if they are approaching their next seat selection and want to gain knowledge from the experiences of past trainee solicitors.

# Chapter 2: Employability and Careers

This chapter is tackled by John Watkins, the Director of Employability at The University of Law. The aim of this chapter is to breakdown the core of employability in the legal sector and the future challenges aspiring solicitors might face and how to overcome it.

### Background

"As we approach the end of 2020 and, for aspiring solicitors, the last few years of the Legal Practice Course in its current form, it is interesting to reflect on the twenty-seven years since its launch back in 1993. But it was not just the LPC that arrived that year: 1993 also saw the formation of the Careers Service at the then College of Law.

### In numbers:

There have been huge changes in the legal profession during this period. These changes include:

i. 61,329 to 143,167 - increase in number of solicitors with Practising Certificates (PC) (76,019 to 188,868 on the roll).
ii. 51% to 30% - fall in partners as a proportion of PC holders in private practice.
iii. 82% to 66% - drop in PC holders working in private practice as in-house grows.
iv. 28% to 51% - increase in women as a % of PC holders.
v. 2% to 14% - increase in ethnic minority solicitors as a % of PC holders.
vi. 3,689 to 5,811 - increase in the number of trainee solicitors registered.
vii. 54% to 65% - increase in women as a % of trainee solicitors.

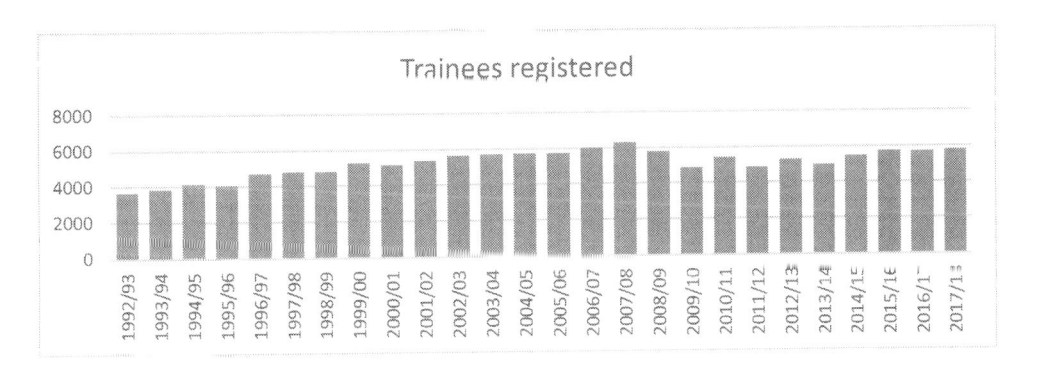

## Changes in the workplace, in the student body and Future Trainee Solicitors:

The legal profession has grown and become increasingly diverse - recruitment comes from a wider pool of talent - albeit that candidates may emerge from higher education having invested more in their degrees or foregone university altogether and followed the apprenticeship route. There is geographical and social mobility too as those with no history of the profession in their family are encouraged to access it. Suits still prevail, wigs still worn but 'business casual' and dress down days are now common.

The nature of the work done has undergone a monumental shift in the last two decades. IT has revolutionised the way we work – no one had email on their phone in the early 90s, messages were far from instant and often hand-delivered before the emergence of the facsimile. Artificial Intelligence is now promising to fundamentally change the early career journey which was so heavily reliant on a hands-on grounding. Law firms are more global now and certainly more commercially driven - especially since the 2008 crash - leading not only to a push for efficiencies through new systems, but new ways of working too. Limited liability partnerships are the norm, and there have also been increases in competition brought about by changes in the regulation of the legal services market.

And how have the young lawyers, entering the profession changed over the years? Much is said about the new generation being tech-savvy digital natives, lacking the corporate drive and focus to seek partnership and instead prioritising work-life balance and demanding to feel valued in a workplace that embraces sustainability.

How much, and the extent to which, any of this is true is debatable. Certainly, newer generations of lawyers are likely to be in the workplace for a considerable time - retirement may soon be a concept that used to exist, much like snowflakes used to be the highlight of the winter months. And while navigating a more competitive, changing and possibly demanding working environment, expectations extend to being successful in other spheres of their life too. Loyalty (which some may see as a positive and others the reverse) has less pertinence as employees are more willing not only to move jobs but to re-train in a completely new field.

**So, what of the Careers Service, founded all those years ago:**

There are some new features – a merger with our award-winning Pro Bono department to form an Employability Service, more focus on employability skills and planning a career as Employability for Life brings awareness to the personal financial, emotional and relational challenges which intertwine with the professional role. Some aspects remain unchanged - one-to-one advice and guidance, support to navigate recruitment processes, interaction with employers and our mentoring scheme.

**The Mentoring Scheme at The University of Law:**

It was launched in 1997 - a one-to-one non-judgmental relationship in which an individual mentor gives his or her time to support and encourage another. Nine mentors supported students on our Chester campus in Year 1 but it quickly expanded nationally to become one of the largest mentoring schemes of its kind - 7,000 students have now been mentored by members of the legal profession! Annual surveys confirm the impact:

i. 82% of students felt more confident in their choice of career.
ii. 79% saw how their course at the university related to practice.

**Employability for Life**

**Lifelong learning – to maintain motivation and ensure skills are up to date:**

The securing of an entry role is just the start of your career journey. It is likely to span many decades, contain many highs and lows, with the professional elements weaving into the personal features to form your life. This is not often appreciated at the outset - and why would it be. Most students are early into their adult life and thoughts of commitments and priorities further down the line are legitimately some way behind the more immediate short-term opportunities and challenges.

So, whilst the focus at university can remain that first run of the ladder, perhaps it would be wise to at least register that the emphasis will subsequently change to arguably more important and more critical decisions. Interestingly, you might even make decisions on which institution to study at based on the commitment to providing support to you when you seek assistance in deciding on career moves (or whether to stay), the optimal timing and other common post qualification dilemmas.

There are many very good training courses provided by employers or available privately - they allow networking and peer interaction which is valuable and often enhances learning. However, as careers progress, the need to refine, develop and enhance skills is often critical - particularly if new roles are aspired to.

These tend to be better addressed on a one-to-one basis than in a group setting for there are likely to be admissions of relative weakness and some openness about personal and professional ambitions which are easier to share with a single confidant.

It is not uncommon for students to be eligible for ongoing free support in their endeavours to secure initial employment after completing their course. But what might happen further down the line?

An admission of thoughts to your employer that you are assessing your future options comes with risks - they may see you as not loyal and less committed to a longer-term career - and recruitment agents are ultimately paid by an employer rather than candidates. Universities commitment to students is to provide impartial advice; it is a very distinctive and important feature. Might it have a part to play?

Alumni are likely to value access to advice on subsequent career decision-making, such as:

i. Seeking a role with a different employer.
ii. Taking a career break/sabbatical.
iii. Returning to work after a break.
iv. Changing career direction.

Given that this moves way beyond the initial navigation into the workplace and has the prospect for adding measurable support, it would not be unreasonable if this involved an agreed fee for a series of consultations - career coaching adds value.

Amongst the skills that most often need refinement and improvement are the following:

i. Time management.
ii. Presentation skills.
iii. Team leadership.
iv. Effective networking.
v. Conflict resolution.
vi. Delegation.

**Life wide insight on challenges that affect professional or personal success:**

A career can last for anything up to fifty years and some will even go beyond that. Consider what might happen in that time period:

i. Relationships; marriage, divorce, partnership, estrangement.
ii. Family; births, deaths, support, fall-outs.
iii. Caring responsibilities; children, grandchildren, parents.
iv. Health; your own and others; mental and physical.
v. Finance; mortgage, debts, investments, pension, life insurance.
vi. Property; rental, home ownership, shared arrangement.

The professional journey takes place alongside the personal highs and lows - the two are inextricably linked. We cannot be experts on everything, so we need to have the willingness to source support from those that do. This may be medical professionals, disability support, mental health advisers, professional financial advisers, relationship counsellors or conciliation/mediation services.

For early exposure to areas which may not affect students themselves initially, there is encouragement to participate in Pro Bono schemes and/or volunteering where a number of these real-life issues are encountered, and the implications better understood.

**The 2020 impact:**

This life wide concept has taken a dramatic turn in 2020, with workers trying to undertake their duties from home whilst also responsible for caring - young and old - including home-schooling for a period of time.

Employers have had to develop an understanding of the multiple priorities and be supportive of those needing to work different hours to fulfil all of their commitments. The complexities of one's personal life have often been left at home, even if the emotional impact has been evident in an office environment. In 2020 these barriers have come down.

The 2020 professional needs to be agile and a confident virtual operator. The 2020 manager needs to be understanding, realistic, imaginative and more emotionally intelligent than ever before.

**The Resilience Conundrum:**

One of the most common responses to the question asked of employers about new employee's limitations is 'a lack of resilience'. In fairness, inexperienced workers will often have a lack of lots of things as, by definition, they have had minimal exposure. Nonetheless 'resilience' has even started to trump 'commercial awareness' as the missing ingredient and is therefore emerging as an area of real focus.

There are some arguments that cite the 'snowflake generation' and multiple references to the schooling system being too rewarding. However, there has been far less attention on the employers who are managing these individuals, and this is where I think lessons can be learned.

Firstly, there needs to be consideration about the coaching, support and on-the-job training for new staff. In discussions with new employees, I find that management is generally liked and respected, but there was a wish for a little more time to be devoted to them - feedback, recognition and involvement were the most commonly used words. Many, however, thought it inadvisable to make too much of this for fear of appearing to be struggling.

In an era of increased apprenticeship numbers, the feedback was similar, but starker with the wish for more support explained in honest terms. Those with minimal prior work experience and often limited technical knowledge at the outset recognised, there was a huge amount to learn. The learning curve is understandably far greater for an apprentice than a graduate starter and it is arguably even more difficult for such an individual to speak up. Whilst conceptually the need to offer enhanced support was common sense, only a modest percentage of employers appear to have really understood this and delivered on a proportionate response. Thus, the provision of adequate support is infrequently common practice.

So, lack of resilience may be partly attributable to insufficient support to equip employees with awareness and tools to deal with challenges. The second consideration is the different take on the meaning of resilience and assessment of it. A pre-course questionnaire in advance of an employer requested training session on resilience asked for self-assessment of employability skills as defined by the Confederation of British Industry.

Business and commercial awareness scored relatively low, an outcome very much aligned with employers' perspective on the development of this attribute. However, positive attitude (most closely reconcilable to resilience) was far and away the highest scorer - any self-assessment of less than nine out of ten was rare and exceptional. It is admirable that there is such self-belief and I suspect that employers would rate this area higher than many others (especially if they had robust recruitment processes). It is, though, unlikely that it would be anywhere near the aforementioned heights.

There is an expectation gap on what a positive attitude comprises, and the resulting shortfall is perhaps being equated with a lack of resilience. It may be further influenced by generational differences – the norm of long, hard hours being all part of the desired route to partnership replaced by a new perspective.

Partnership is not necessarily the goal (risk versus reward?), money is viewed differently (there are debts, home ownership is not a realistic ambition), careers are longer (retirement age increasing and pensions not as generous). Plus, the environment and climate change are exercising the mind much more.

The solutions - better preparation for degrees of failure through the schooling process, appreciation from employer and employee that developing some workplace skills is very much a combined effort, early and detailed dialogue on what is actually meant and expected by certain key terms, and a better understanding of the motivations of new entrants to the workplace. It will require widespread resilience to achieve!

## Advice for Mature Students (and valuable insight for those competing against them):

Employers are increasingly positive about the opportunity to recruit mature students for graduate level roles.

However, not all of them follow this through and offer roles. You can look at case studies to see who is featured and what they say about their journey. You can also attend Careers Fairs and other events to ask existing staff. Even if the words are positive you might wonder why none of the junior representatives are mature!

For most mature students the following are generally seen as advantageous:

i. Decision to study reflects a positive, conscious commitment which is seen as reassuring and demonstrates focus.
ii. Life experiences will have developed a range of skills and exposure to a wide range of situations and people.
iii. Any prior work experience, even in an unrelated field, provides an awareness of the workplace and its nuances (commuting, performance reviews, use of IT in a business context, diversity of staff, customer/client interaction).
iv. Awareness of commercial realities is often strong; either from experience in a business environment and/or evaluating the merits (return on investment) from embarking on a course of study.

The key requirement for mature students is to highlight the advantages above and ensure that through applications, CV's and interviews that these relative strengths are emphasised.

Employers are not able to discriminate on the basis of age and thus the potential disadvantages need to be countered without ever actually being formally questioned:

i. How will you react to being managed by someone much younger?
ii. How will our clients react to a junior member of staff being older than those they have encountered previously?

Both these 'fears' can be addressed proactively by giving examples of scenarios in the past where there has been no problem at all (or even better, that something positive has resulted).

The other question in the mind of the recruiter (which again is difficult to ask without risk of discrimination) is:

How will this person react when their younger manager is about to make a big mistake?
i. They would step in and use the advantage of experience to prevent the big mistake from happening.
ii. They would stand back and recognise that it is not their place to interfere and allow the big mistake to happen.

Answer i - prevents the big mistake but risks undermining the manager and damaging your relationship and impacting on other colleagues too.

Answer ii - prevents the relationship damage (unless the manager thinks you have intentionally let them fail) but means that a big mistake happens.

This is the crux of the challenge for mature students. If employers are thinking that there is no good answer in the scenario above, then they might default to favouring other candidates (consciously or unconsciously).

Thus, the mature student must find a way to weave into their application/interview that they have such judgment and experience to know how to handle such a situation. Essentially, it depends on the individual, the nature of the relationship, whether the big mistake is easily rectified or beyond repair.

## Personal finance:

There is a whole industry involved in helping people with their personal finances and there is no substitute for professional advice. It may, however, stimulate some thoughts and should act as a catalyst for pro-active management of your personal obligations.

**Student loan (via Student finance)**
**(Using example of English/Welsh based student - different for Scotland/NI):**

The assumption is that you have taken out a student loan for an undergraduate and/or a postgraduate course, subject to various eligibility criteria. There are a number of complicated elements, but at a very high level:

i. Loans accrue interest from the first day of the course until the loan is repaid; the interest rate being RPI +3% (updated each September).
ii. You are due to make repayments from April after you complete or withdraw from your course if you are earning above the repayment threshold for your type of loan.
iii. You pay 9% of your income over the UG threshold and 6% for the PG threshold.
iv. Your employer will make deductions from your pay, so you need not do anything unless you are self-employed where you will complete a Self-Assessment tax return.

**Other loans:**

i. Where you have taken out other loans you will be bound by their terms.
ii. These tend not to have repayment thresholds; you must repay whatever your level of earnings or indeed if you are not earning at all.

**What this means:**

i. You need to budget for the repayments.
ii. You should factor the commitment into your decision-making, particularly major financial considerations; property, education, healthcare, career options.

**Pension planning:**

It is never too early to start putting money aside for the future. Again, there is a wealth of advice around a huge variety of options, so the simple message is to be proactive and take time to fully assess your strategy. Clearly, the greater the 'sacrifice' for the longer-term, the lower the disposable income available in the short-term.

**Your credit history:**

Banks or other lenders (i.e. providers of contracted services such as mobile phones) use your credit history to assess the risk of lending to you (often giving you a 'credit score'). Many companies will choose not to lend to you if you have not always managed your credit well and do not have a good credit rating, while others might lend but charge you a higher rate of interest or offer you a smaller amount of credit. It only relates to your activity - if parents have paid your bills on time for many years that has no impact on your credit rating (likewise if they have missed payments).

A credit report typically includes:

i. A list of your credit accounts. This includes bank and credit card accounts as well as other credit arrangements such as outstanding loan agreements or utility company debts. They will show whether you have made repayments on time and in full. Items such as missed or late payments or defaults will stay on your credit report for at least six years.
ii. Details of any people who are financially linked to you, for example, because you have taken out joint credit.
iii. Public record information - I.e. County Court Judgments, house repossessions, bankruptcies and individual voluntary arrangements, which stay on your report for at least six years.
iv. Your current account provider, but only details of overdrafts.
v. If you have committed a fraud, or someone has stolen your identity and committed fraud, this will be held on your file under the CIFAS section.

Employers and landlords can also check your credit report, although they will usually only see public record information such as electoral register information, insolvency records and County Court Judgements.

Repeatedly applying for credit can harm your chances of getting credit, because lots of credit searches might indicate you are having problems.

If you are applying for a loan, mortgage, credit card or other borrowing then it might be a good idea to check your credit report first. It is often worth getting a copy from all three main credit reference agencies (CRAs) as they might have different information from different credit providers. All CRAs have a statutory obligation to provide you with a copy of your credit report for free. You can access the report online or by asking for a written copy. You can check your credit report as often as you like and it will not affect your credit rating or credit score.

**What can you do:**

Primarily it is about living within your means and being disciplined and well organised in settling debts. However, consider also other tactics, including:

i. Put things into your name so that timely payments are benefitting your credit history.
ii. Register on the electoral roll as you will find it much harder to get credit if not.
iii. Bear in mind that lenders feel more comfortable if they see evidence that you have lived at one address for a considerable period.
iv. Cancel unused credit cards."

# Chapter 3: Working in Different Departments

If you are an aspiring solicitor or a trainee solicitor rotating seats, then this chapter might be of interest to you. The objective of this section is to break down the different departments in a commercial law firm by sharing the insight of trainee solicitors and qualified solicitors who undertook seats in those teams. A small caveat - seats vary from firm to firm and this is meant to be a taster of what to expect rather than a complete guide to every commercial law firm. In no particular order, departments covered in this section by trainee solicitors include:

- Banking
- Capital Markets and Derivatives
- Corporate
- Construction
- Commercial Litigation
- Derivatives
- Financial Regulation
- Funds
- Intellectual Property
- Knowledge Lawyer
- Pensions
- Restructuring and Insolvency
- Real Estate
- Technology, Media and Telecommunications (also known as TMT)
- Tax
- Trade and Export Finance

**Corporate, Derivatives and Banking at Linklaters with Ex-Associate Deepti Patankar**

**About Deepti's Experience:**

"A trainee solicitors' job is to learn as much as possible from her principal and those around her who have more knowledge and experience. In order to do that, a trainee solicitor is given lots of discrete tasks - everything from scanning, printing, proof reading to drafting minor letters/notices, drafting emails to clients and deal project management falls in the lap of a trainee solicitor.

A trainee solicitor also gets to attend several meetings and conference calls with clients and lawyers on the other side of the deal. All of these are learning opportunities for a trainee solicitor to soak up not only how law and contracts work but also how commercial agreements and client service is conducted.

What I enjoyed the most was the constant learning on the job and seeing how the theoretical knowledge of the law translates into practical real-life solutions. And also, the fact that my deals were large, usually multinational and often making it to the front page of The Financial Times. This was the only glamorous part of the job!

I trained at Linklaters and their emphasis on training and coaching was fantastic. The firm has extremely high standards - the lawyers who work there are required to produce meticulous work, in both form and substance. When you train at a place like Linklaters you cannot help but absorb these qualities and they stand you in good stead wherever else you go. Being surrounded by smart people also meant that I had to raise my game. I enjoyed the competition and I truly believe it helped me become a better professional.

Linklaters focuses on huge deals for premium clients. They pride themselves on their blue-chip clients and have a strong culture built on excellence and integrity. Training at Linklaters means long hours and hard work because your work has to be of the highest quality. You are surrounded by so many smart and competent people, it was almost frightening but as I said before, it helped me raise my game. Linklaters also had a great social calendar for their trainee solicitors, and they invested quite a fair amount in organising parties and events for us - this was a bonus!

**The Corporate Seat at Linklaters:**

I was placed in the public M&A team for my first seat at Linklaters. During my time in the Corporate seat, I got to experience some large M&A deals and share issues to investors. As a trainee solicitor, I was assigned tasks which mostly included drafting board minutes and resolutions for shareholders, notices to investors, reviewing prospectus for share rights and helping with due diligence of target companies.

I worked extremely long hours in this seat due to the size of the deals we were working on. This is very common for corporate seats because the corporate team is usually the nerve centre for any M&A deal and co-ordinates all other departments and jurisdictions. Deals are usually multinational. Time difference across jurisdictions in international deals also adds to the long hours.

Corporate M&A is very process driven. Trainee solicitors are assigned the task of collecting/coordinating various pieces of paper without which a deal cannot be completed. This requires a trainee solicitor to be super organised and tenacious. You will find yourself chasing people who are far more senior than you for these papers so you will learn to manage upwards. One can also expect to learn the processes that govern how a company is run under the Companies Act. You will be asked to draft notices, letters, shareholder resolutions and board minutes. You will also find yourself doing due diligence on M&A target companies.

The best corporate lawyers have a real and practical outlook which their clients appreciate. They know how the law works very well but are able to apply it to the real-world problem and come up with a commercially suitable answer. You have to be comfortable with client pressure and changing situations. You have to be able to juggle multiple tasks and you have to be super organised and structured.

**The Banking Seat at Linklaters:**

Banking is the second biggest department of Linklaters. My clients were usually banks who are looking to lend money to a company for various uses such as acquisitions and working capital. I did part of my Banking seat in our Moscow office where we worked on trade finance deals for Russian state companies.

My fourth seat was also in banking but in Dubai where you have Islamic finance which is super fascinating. Banking is another transactional seat, so most of my time was spent on calls and meetings where my principal would be negotiating lending documents on behalf of some bank or borrower. We would then draft up the results of these negotiations and send them across to both sides for their final agreement.

Hours are generally quite long in this seat due to the time pressure for getting the deals done quickly. In banking, you can expect to assist with drafting lending agreements, security documents (such as charges, mortgages and pledges) and getting them registered with the right government authority, conducting security reviews for lenders and ending enforcement notices to borrowers.

As a trainee solicitor, you will also be responsible for collecting condition precedent documents for a deal to complete. This involved coordinating with various other law firms or internal departments such as Tax, IP and Employment. A highlight for me was asset finance and real estate finance, which are all part of the banking seat and are huge amounts of fun! You get to see how airplanes and yachts are bought and sold and how they are funded.

In Dubai, their lending and security laws were not as fully developed as in the UK. I had a particularly interesting visit to a port authority in some dusty part of old Dubai, where I was trying to convince the authorities that my clients, the banks, could take over the ship of the borrower!

**The Derivatives Seat at Linklaters:**

My derivatives seat was very different from corporate and banking seats in that the deals are generally bespoke, smaller in size with very little involvement of other departments and highly complex. Deals are usually slower paced due to the complexity and smaller in size (monetary terms). There is a lot of training in the early part of the seat, much more than in corporate and banking. There is an entire vocabulary around ISDA and derivatives that one needs to understand and get comfortable with before one can make a meaningful contribution. Because the deal size is much smaller in derivatives, you get early client contact and the ability to draft documents. The pace is slower, which can mean some 6pm finishes!

You can expect to deal with your clients one-to-one in derivatives. You get to draft and negotiate swaps, options and other financial instruments. The best aspect was that I really felt like I was exercising my brain trying to get my head around complex financial instruments. There can be a lot of free drafting (i.e. without any precedents) involved which is fun and creative!

This seat would suit someone who likes attention to details and intellectual exercises. Some of the structured products require a bit of imagination to understand because they are complex. The people interaction element is also significantly lesser than in corporate and banking, so it suits introverts."

## Real Estate at Trowers & Hamlins with Trainee Solicitor Sajeed Jamal

### About Sajeed's Experience:

"I was always one of those children who would read the fine print. Whether it would be the cereal box at breakfast or the pack of Panini stickers on the playground, so you could say it started from childhood! On a serious note, I became interested in the law, when starting my A-Levels. Prior to A-Levels, I did not even know that commercial law even existed! I was very naïve. I thought all law was just criminal and I had no idea about commercial law. My A-Level law teacher was very inspirational and she encouraged me to do law at undergraduate level. Her sister was a corporate lawyer, and that is when the notion of working as a commercial solicitor at an international law firm first came into my mind.

Being someone who was always interested in business, I knew that was what I wanted to go into, but I was also interested in the humanities. In fact, I loved history. I felt that reading for a law degree in a way combined all of those subjects nicely and would provide for a solid grounding for any career. Once I finished my A-levels, a career as a lawyer was something I was dead set on. Prior to those two years, I did not know what I wanted to do - after those two years, I just wanted to be a lawyer!

Trowers & Hamlins was a firm I had my eye on from the very start after, after undertaking my research. I have always been interested in the Middle East. Trowers & Hamlins are one of the market-leading firms in the region having been there since the 1950s. Hence, they have worked on some of the largest and most ground-breaking projects and deals in the MENA region, many of which are 'first-in-country' or 'first-in-region' matters.

Secondly, Trowers & Hamlins have an enviable reputation in the real estate sector and for their work in the built environment, along with a top-tier public sector and Islamic finance practice. All of these factors made me want to apply to Trowers & Hamlins.

I then applied and attended an open day at Trowers & Hamlins, and I was truly shocked with how down to earth and approachable the people were. The open day was so refreshing compared to previous open days. It was one of those open days where I felt no awkwardness and had no imposter syndrome! I realised straight away Trowers & Hamlins was different in its approach for an international law firm. Trowers & Hamlins is known for being unique, open and having a friendly culture.

I felt that the firm values resonated with my own. I also felt my individuality would be seen as a strength. There genuinely is no 'Trowers type'. It is a firm that genuinely cares about diversity, inclusion, and individuality. I felt it is a place where I see myself could thrive - as I could just be myself.

After undertaking the vacation scheme, I could see myself working alongside the people I met. Secondly, whilst on the scheme, I saw that diversity is very real at Trowers & Hamlins, it permeated throughout the firm. As a BAME applicant, this just further appealed to me.

**The Real Estate seat at Trowers & Hamlins:**

As a trainee solicitor, you have a lot of responsibility. It is one of those seats that you assist on all elements of a matter. From inception to conclusion. Trainee solicitors are given files to manage from the start. This could be working on a licence to alter for a refit, working on a complicated substation lease, or assisting with property due diligence of an international corporate deal.

Luckily, at Trowers & Hamlins we are treated given real responsibility and extensive client contact (obviously we are supervised!) but are involved in all aspects of a transaction. This could be replies to standard enquiries, drafting documents, reviewing the landlord's title to the property or taking instructions from a client.

The most interesting deal I have worked on so far was dealing with a well-known international retailer outlet who wish to renew their existing lease on one of their flagship stores. I assisted with negotiating the heads of terms and assisted with the negotiation of an agreement for lease. I also coordinated the exchange and once all their conditions had been satisfied, we managed to complete within the requisite timeframe. This allowed the retailer to continue to occupy the premises whilst a number of refurbishment works were taking place, thus saving and avoiding the fiasco of the store having to be closed for a long duration.

I have always thought that I would be a transactional lawyer, but after undertaking a few vacation schemes and being a paralegal in contentious and non-contentious work, I realised I do enjoy contentious work as well. Therefore, I had taken the view that I needed to have a real open mind in my training contract and not decide to early on. I read countless times, where someone wanted to be a corporate lawyer but then they became a planning lawyer because they enjoyed that seat so much.

I think it is important to just learn and develop as much as possible and have an open mind, so when I do qualify, I am a very competent newly qualified solicitor. I do not want to say I wish to be such a corporate lawyer and then in my mind subconsciously be affected by that thought process and not give my hundred percent in any seat. So, I am sitting on the fence with this question! What I can say is that I would probably qualify into an area which has a positive impact on people, makes the world better and where there is a humanistic element to commercial law."

## Capital Markets and Derivatives at CMS with Trainee Solicitor Louise Formisano

### About Louise's Experience:

"Like the stereotypical lawyer, I had an interest in law from a youngish age. I remember attending a careers evening in secondary school - what I took away from it was that as a lawyer, I could play a part in so many aspects of everyday life. Once I got to university, attended more firm events and made more of an effort into researching into the career, it really firmed the idea in my head that a career in law is impactful, important and can be very rewarding.

I first applied just after the merger in 2017, as it was clear that this was shaking up the legal world and could be interesting to be a part of. After I was rejected, I put the idea of applying to bed until I graduated and started my LPC the following year. I had decided that I did not actually want to apply for such a large firm, reflected in my applications to other mid-sized city firms, but ended up putting CMS back into the application mix anyway as I knew that there was a large variety of departments, many with high rankings within their respective industries. It was not until after I had completed the assessment centre did I realise how much I thought that this firm was for me - the trainee solicitors, partners and HR teams that I met on the day were so welcoming and genuine, and I felt like I could really visualise myself at the firm.

### The Capital Markets and Derivatives seat at CMS:

I have had lots of experience drafting and negotiating in this seat. Compared to my peers, I think that I have escaped a lot of the 'grunt work', such as filling out forms, de-registering security and putting together condition precedent lists. Instead, I have kindly been given a lot of explanation and training by the other members of the team - associates through to partners - enabling me to access a completely new and technical area of law that is never really encountered by the average person. Frequent communication with key clients has meant that I have begun to understand these clients' needs specifically and can continue to do repeat work for them with more and more autonomy.

Capital Markets and Derivatives was a bit of a wild card as my first seat, but I can definitely see myself happy to qualify here. I still have an interest in our Energy teams, specifically Oil and Gas, as well as the Funds and Indirect Real Assets team. However, I have been given the opportunity to second to Goldman Sachs in my next seat, which is another Capital Markets seat, which will definitely boost my confidence in this area and give a whole new perspective to the work I have been undertaking so far.

Work wise there is generally always a negotiation going on. We work with ISDA Schedules, Credit Support Annexes and Global Master Repurchase Agreements mostly (I know, a mouthful!). With our key clients, they are constantly making these agreements with other parties and these are some of the most important agreements that you have never heard of! They are used by nearly every bank, hedge fund and corporate in the world in order to raise capital or cover a short position.

I have also been drafting a lot of pricing supplements. Banks issue 'securities' which are a type of investment you can buy, hold or sell, and on maturity you will get a pay-out based on the derivative (i.e. the value of the pay-out is derived from another asset, such as an index or shares). A pricing supplement accompanies these issues to include the terms and conditions relevant to the issue.

I have also been getting involved with reviewing legal opinions, drafting board minutes and undertaking research tasks, which are important to get right in the trainee solicitor role, but fortunately I have not been swamped with this work during this seat."

**Banking at Ashurst with Trainee Solicitor Sofia Aslam**

**About Sofia's Experience:**

"So far my seats have been fine. A lot of people in the City are used to being good at everything, and when you are in an environment where everything is new that just does not happen. Think of it all as development - any time you are given criticism, you have learnt something. Treat it like an opportunity and you will benefit!

Networking is really important - knowing the right people to reach out to for the right things can help make your own career progress really well! There are different ways to build on this, I have always found that networking is quite natural when you have commonalities with people but sometimes you have to force yourself out of your comfort zone to speak to people that you would not ordinarily.

In my opinion, a willingness to learn is the biggest skill that makes a good trainee solicitor! Attention to detail does not hurt either - if you do all the small things that you are assigned well, that builds a really good image of you, and you might end up getting access to better opportunities.

If you are already a trainee solicitor to ensure you are continuously developing - set some goals at the beginning of each seat and every month think about whether you have done anything to achieve those goals, either at work or outside of work.

**The Banking seat at Ashurst:**

Banking - very fast paced and might be described as a 'baptism of fire' which is very true but really helps you develop core transactional and organisational skills that can be transferred to any other team. You are on deals helping different clients get finance for various different reasons.

This, as a trainee solicitor, means negotiating documents that need to be in place in order for the loan to be granted (conditions precedent). The negotiation is often through circulating comments on draft documents that have been circulated to you by lawyers on the other side, but you also have to lead calls to discuss anything outstanding. It is your job to be on top of what needs to be done.

In a Banking seat, you have to be pretty deadline driven - the pace is quite fast and turnaround on deals is usually on a tight time frame. I think you have to be good at managing lots of different responsibilities and deals as they will all be at different stages and you have to know what still needs to be done. Once you have done a deal, you pretty much know the structure of them.

One tip I could advise trainee solicitors moving onto this seat is to make to-do lists at the start of each day; you add the most value when you know where things are. Do not be afraid to ask questions but try to be independent and progress ancillary documents as much as you can."

## **Restructuring and Insolvency at Pinsent Masons with Trainee Solicitor Jade Naylor**

### **About Jade's Experience:**

"Having just started my role as a paralegal within the firm I knew instantly that Pinsent Masons was a place where I would want to do my training contract. A partner once said to me that they have been with Pinsent Masons for so long because of the people, the clients and the innovation, and that is completely right. The people are welcoming, down-to-earth and everyone is treated with respect no matter what level or stage of your career you are at. The firm has a global outlook, working with international clients but still values its local community ties whether that is through matter-related work or CSR initiatives and that was also important to me.

### **The Restructuring and Insolvency Seat at Pinsent Masons:**

In my first weeks I was required to visit a client's home to get documents signed. I was nervous as I had only just started as a trainee solicitor and I took three spare copies of the documents just in case I made a mistake as I could not go back to the office to print any more. It was a great experience meeting a client on my own and in their home. It was also quite challenging as I had to keep the conversation going, whilst ensuring all the documents were signed and that I was witnessing them correctly.

Every day/week is different in restructuring which is what I really enjoyed. I did a lot of work around companies going into administration. There are two routes to enter administration; the out-of-court and the in-court route and I was able to experience both. I was able to assist with the drafting of the documents for the court route and also go with my supervisor to the hearing.

With the out-of-court route you still need to draft court documents and file documents with the court and so you still need to adhere to the court cut off times which makes it extremely fast-paced. Therefore, being prepared and having all your documents ready to go is key. A restructuring seat is technical and you will also spend time researching, namely around the Insolvency Act. You can also expect transactional work when working on pre-pack deals, and again these are fast-paced. If you are looking for an area that is fast-paced and no two days are the same, then restructuring is a great seat to do.

This seat is a fast-paced environment which is why great organisation and preparation is key. Restructuring crosses over into many different areas of law so understanding Corporate law, M&A, Property law and Banking will greatly assist you throughout the seat.

Through completing this seat my attention to detail has definitely improved. The ability to produce high-quality work with little or no errors to a tight deadline is a great skill that I have learnt during my restructuring seat. I have also learnt how to work under pressure and how to relieve that pressure by being organised and proactive.

In terms of tips, I think this applies to all trainee solicitors starting a seat rather than specifically restructuring. I would say be open-minded, what you think you might not like you might end up enjoying and vice versa. Be proactive and go into the seat with a 'can-do' attitude.

If you are not sure about something, then ask questions! Most of the time it is easily fixable, but in a seat like restructuring where it is fast-paced, it could be crucial."

## Trade & Export Finance, Commercial Litigation, and Financial Services Regulatory/Ali Siddiqui, Associate at CMS and Former Trainee Solicitor at Accutrainee Limited

**About Ali's Experience:**

"A day can vary from having me be one step away from twiddling my thumbs to suddenly doing a fifteen-hour shift with little advance notice. It depends on how many of the transactions I am working on are 'live' that week and how my team's work pipeline is looking. Generally, I am working on about two transactions at a time, most of which involves drafting or amending transaction documents, liaising with a mid-level associate and partner, responding to emails from the client or local counsel.

What I really like is the process of taking a concept or arrangement that has been agreed between the parties and then reflecting it in a contract with language as clearly and unambiguously as possible. It is the bread-and-butter of solicitor work, really - understanding a complex concept and then drafting wording to give effect to it legally. I find the end result of this quite satisfying.

What has been potentially challenging has been the unpredictability that comes with working in private practice (particularly in Finance). As I said, there is often no telling when you will be needed to suddenly do a 9am to midnight and beyond. Sometimes a day is quiet until 5:30pm, and then the work begins!

Internally, I enjoy getting involved with the BAME Network and Muslim Network, as well as the accelerator programme that the firm runs. This naturally expands my connections. Externally, I am often approached on LinkedIn by paralegals applying for training contracts, and so my network expands at the junior end as well.

**The Trade and Export Finance seat at Sullivan & Worcester (via Accutrainee Limited):**

In this seat I completed:

i. Drafting and updating of Conditions Precedent checklists.
ii. Loan agreements.
iii. Receivables purchase agreements.
iv. Security agreements.
v. Signing instructions.
vi. Legal opinions (both capacity and enforceability).
vii. Fee proposals
viii. Engagement letters.
ix. Fee proposal requests to local counsel and pitches - all in the context of trade and supply-chain financing (a relatively niche area of debt finance).

The seat was drafting-heavy with some research and occasional negotiation with the counterparty's counsel (mainly via email and comments on documents).

The best aspect of this seat was that it was a good experience and very representative of what working as a transactional lawyer is like. High level of responsibility. In my opinion, this seat requires an extremely high level of attention to detail. What you may perceive as high level is most likely not high enough by lawyer standards. In addition to this, you need a positive attitude, good drafting skills, command of language, clear communication, and good research skills.

Tips I would advise for this seat are to be proactive and volunteer for work. However, equally, try to do so without going overboard and over-promising (this can be a difficult balance). Always assume that things will take a bit longer than you think they will, especially if legal blacklines (comparison documents) are involved. And, when it can seem like you are involved in a series of discrete tasks, make sure to take a step back and think about the bigger picture; the transaction as a whole. This will help you have a better understanding of what you are doing, while avoiding mistakes.

**The Commercial Litigation seat at William Grace (via Accutrainee Limited):**

My average week in this seat generally involved drafting correspondence to the opposing party's solicitors and reviewing any incoming correspondence from them. This drafting was often in preparation for a mediation. I also compiled bundles, investigated evidence provided by clients and formed an initial view as to the legal position, and drafted pre-action letters, requests for further information, and a report of preliminary advice. Additionally, I researched relevant steps to be taken in the run-up to a Case Management Conference, and prepared and filed a Directions Questionnaire and Costs Budget.

Preparing for the mediation included:

i. Attending strategy meetings with clients and counsel.
ii. Preparing and filing a notice of application for an extension of stay on proceedings.
iii. Drafting and negotiating NDAs in relation to company valuations.
iv. Liaising with a valuation expert and reviewing financial statements.

My favourite aspect of this seat was that the hours were generally very good. There was a high level of responsibility (particularly via being allowed to have a first go at drafting the legal correspondence, which I understand would not usually be a trainee task). I developed a good relationship with the client on an on-going case. I gained a thorough understanding of NDAs and attended client meetings with the valuation expert. In my opinion, this seat again requires a very high level of attention to detail, an ability to damage-mitigate if mistakes are made, good research skills, organisational skills, and communication skills (largely written).

I would say this seat suits someone who is very organised and enjoys observing the game-playing and strategising of the parties in dispute. It is definitely not for someone who likes mooting and courtroom advocacy; you will be disappointed if you have that in mind!

Tips I would advise for this seat is to try and get a good understanding of all stages of the litigation so far (if you are joining mid-case). As ever, do not be afraid to ask when you are not sure (provided you have had a go first). Try to offer your thoughts on strategy where possible/relevant.

**The Financial Regulation seat at Promontory Financial Group, an IBM Company (via Accutrainee Limited):**

I learnt a lot about the Senior Managers & Certification Regime and the FCA handbook. I also got involved in the in-house legal side of things, which included drafting different types of engagement letters and otherwise assisting in the migration of before a Transfer-of-Business contracts from Promontory to IBM.

During this seat, I assisted in preparing a major retail bank's various FCA-solo-regulated entities for the implementation of the Senior Managers & Certification Regime before 9 December 2019.

Responsibilities included:

i. Understanding each entity's and the overall groups corporate governance and drafting Management Responsibility Maps for each entity.

ii. Drafting rationales for the appointment of individual senior managers to allocated functions within each entity and preparing development plans and gap analyses in support of these.
iii. Liaising with the client in person and via email and conference calls.
iv. Carrying out file reviews into high-risk and medium-risk customers of a bank on which Promontory was conducting a Skilled Person Review. This included an evaluation of weaknesses in systems and controls.
v. Reviewed existing client service contracts against IBM's standard to identify any gaps and obtain IBM approval if necessary. Drafted supply contracts and engagement letters upon approval. Set up matters on the system, including using IBM's pricing tool.

My favourite aspect of this seat was that the team was friendly and approachable. I developed a solid understanding of the regulatory regime in practice. I would advise that good research skills, and an ability to assimilate large volumes of information (in this case the regulation) is required for this seat! One skill I developed was my advisory skills through translating legal concepts into advice for the business.

Overall, I think a good trainee is someone who is enthusiastic and demonstrates that by volunteering for work wherever possible but practicable, has a method for ensuring they are paying a high amount of attention to the detail, is communicative with his or her colleagues and able to manage their workload effectively and is aware of where they can improve while actively takes steps towards doing so."

## Intellectual Property at Simmons & Simmons with Trainee Solicitor Jennifer O'Kane

**About Jennifer's Experience:**

"I studied Biology at the University of Sheffield and became very interested in the overlap between science and law. After some further research, I decided to apply for training contracts at law firms that focussed on the Health Care and Life Sciences sector.

Simmons and Simmons held an open day where I had the opportunity to meet people at the firm and undertake a series of tasks that were similar to the activities carried out on assessment days. We were also given a great tour of the firm's modern art collection! I found that everyone was very friendly and open, which made it easy to get a good feel for the culture of the firm.

**The Intellectual Property seat at Simmons & Simmons:**

The IP team at Simmons & Simmons includes the Patent Litigation, Brands and Commercial IP team, which means it is a broad mixture of contentious and non-contentious work. As part of the Brands team, we work for a number of banks to monitor and prevent infringement of the use of their trademarks. This has been very rewarding as it often results in the shutting down and prevention of fraudulent websites. I have also been involved with a number of patent disputes, which are interesting as you speak to experts in the relevant fields and become knowledgeable about very obscure inventions.

As part of the patents and brands work, trainee solicitors will be expected to draft claim forms and court documents, manage litigation correspondence and research various aspects of intellectual property law. The Commercial IP work often involves intellectual property due diligence, or the drafting of transactional documents such as licensing agreements. Trainee solicitors get involved with all aspects of the transaction and there are often tight deadlines with plenty of opportunities to take ownership and responsibility of discrete aspects of the deal."

## Construction at Pinsent Masons with Lawyer Jason Feng

**About Jason's Experience:**

"During university, I realised pretty early on that I was better at learning on the job than via the textbooks. So, I spent most of my time building up work experience in a variety of legal sectors - from criminal law, to community legal centres, in-house, government and private practice.

Out of all of those experiences, I enjoyed commercial law the most because there is a really active pace of work and learning, and a variety of clients and projects you can get exposed to. I was also fortunate to have worked with great colleagues and find that many people that work in private practice are really intelligent, ambitious and 'switched on'. It is an environment where I feel challenged and presents a variety of opportunities to get involved.

**The Construction seat at Pinsent Masons:**

As a front-end construction lawyer, my average week depends on the projects that I am on. Usually, it is quite reasonable 9am to 6:30pm but there are sometimes multiple late nights/weekends in the urgent stages of projects. One good thing about working in construction is that our clients are generally quite reasonable about timeframes and what can actually be accomplished.

When I am not working on client-related matters, I would be getting involved in business development, knowledge management or preparing training for clients/the team. From late 2019 to early this year, we had intense bushfires across Australia, which destroyed thousands of homes and businesses. My team assisted the contractor that was appointed to coordinate and undertake the first phase of recovery works after the bushfires in NSW.

We carried out the 'normal lawyer work' like helping them understand the contract and potential legal risks. But unlike the typical projects, our involvement was not centred on the commercial outcomes (i.e. making sure that the potential rewards were worth the risk). The focus was really on assisting in areas such as their community engagement processes, how they handle personal data from residents, response to COVID-19 and ongoing communications with the Government.

It was great to see that everyone was working to help recovering communities - definitely one of the 'warm and fuzzy' projects. I think the personal highlights were mostly moments where I started to realise how much I had learned over time and felt like I could actually succeed as a lawyer.

One was running a presentation to clients on a contracts topic and being able to field their questions and actually knowing the answers! The other was being seconded to work within a client's legal team. It was pretty scary not having the safety net of multiple people reviewing my work (like I would in a law firm) but again, super encouraging.

I personally enjoy working on the sector-specific (instead of 'area of law-specific') type of work. There is a real sense that you are understanding and working with clients more collaboratively than in one-off transactions across different sectors. You get exposure to a range of legal issues (contracts, torts, work health and safety, environment, finance, intellectual property and insurance) that affect the sector instead of potentially being pigeonholed into a particular legal area.

The other thing I enjoy is working with practical and logical clients - usually with a commercial, engineering or finance background. They work hard but are also quite reasonable with deadlines and their expectations about outcomes.

Finally, it is good to be able to see a real impact from the work that I have been involved in. Unlike transactions where money moves from one account to another behind the scenes, I can see how a new wharf for cruise liners impacts the local community, or how the road project I worked on saved so much time in peoples' lives.

Skills wise for this seat commercial awareness gets floated around a lot in the legal industry, but I think it is especially important for construction because you are servicing a particular sector. Over the past few years, I have learned the terminology, how businesses operate, where they make their money, the type of work involved (demolition, services, construction, design, maintenance) and the risks/opportunities associated with these different types of work.

On the technical side of things - there is a level of rigour and discipline that I have learned along the way due to the nature of the work - reviewing/drafting two hundred-page contracts, research on fact-heavy cases, and trying to understand the actual commercial documents involved in the deals.

I think the best tip for this seat is to be enthusiastic about learning the actual construction industry itself. Understand the clients, the work that they do and the real impacts on people. Appreciate that these are not just one-off transactions, but quite long-term projects with complex relationships, interesting commercial drivers and lasting results. Once you have this in mind, the legal work itself becomes a lot more interesting and makes more sense."

**Tax at CMS with Trainee Solicitor Lukas Vician**

**About Lukas's Experience:**

"Ever since high school, I knew that I wanted to study law and focused on various legal issues ranging from constitutional law and European Union law to finance and corporate mergers and acquisitions. My Bachelor's degree in The Netherlands naturally pushed me towards European law, tax law and general commercial/corporate law. Even though my Master's degree was mainly in European Union law and tax law, I have kept my focus on the commercial aspects. This proved to be an interesting and valuable background for my training contract, where I have rotated through seats with Corporate Transactions, Project Finance, Funds and am currently working with the tax group.

Ever since I was eleven and actually started to digest what was going on in the world around me, I became interested in politics and surprisingly enjoyed watching the evening news on TV. This passion grew stronger and I was very active with a variety of seminars and discussions at high school, which I helped to co-organise many times. At university, I was involved with the Law Society, mainly with organising the external events, and was also elected its vice-president. I also co-founded the university's law journal.

All of the above sparked my interest in politics in which I have been actively involved, directly or indirectly, ever since. I came very close to running for the European Parliament in Slovakia. While my ambition is to become a lawyer and to build a career in law, politics would have been my other choice in my career path. I would not be surprised if there comes a day when I am able to apply my skills as a corporate lawyer in a political capacity.

Being a good corporate lawyer is not just about knowing the law but also knowing how to apply it with the client's interests in mind. While this may sound cliché, having a strong commercial awareness is a must. A client proceeds with a particular transaction for multiple reasons and if the solicitor understands the reasons, the legal work will be of the highest quality and the client will be comfortable that you know what you are doing. Another key requirement of being a good corporate lawyer is having strong organisational skills. As a purely transactional seat, you will likely be working on multiple transactions at any one time, and these will involve hundreds of documents and dozens of signatory parties. Managing such a large number of stakeholders while providing smooth legal advice and solid document drafts requires corporate solicitors to be alert at all times and to manage their time effectively.

I have always preferred helping to create a business venture to suing one. In the world of business, transactional lawyers try to arrange various deals in ways that avoid litigation, and which make clear the rights and obligations of all parties in the event that something goes wrong. A career in corporate law means playing with the words and being smart enough to ensure that the provisions of an agreement are clear, unambiguous and will not cause problems for the client in the future. It is intellectually demanding and closing a large transaction or preparing a huge structure that deals with all legal aspects properly can be a very rewarding experience. As a trainee solicitor for the past nineteen months, I have been involved in many large successful deals and have found the work to be thoroughly challenging and fulfilling. My wish is for everyone to find their career of interest and to keep following it.

**The Tax seat at CMS:**

The tax team at CMS is part of the wider Corporate practice and as expected, works most closely with other transactional lawyers. However, the team also regularly works with the Real Estate and Tech & Media groups, other practice areas within the firm, and also with the international CMS offices on large cross-border structuring.

Apart from providing support to other departments, the team deals with all aspects of domestic and international tax, including:

i. UK and international mergers, acquisitions, joint ventures and flotations.
ii. Property taxation.
iii. Inward investment into the UK.
iv. UK and cross-border tax consultancy.
v. Finance taxation.
vi. Privatization.
vii. Public-private partnerships and project work.
viii. Employment and income tax.
ix. Trusts and high-net-worth individuals.
x. International investment schemes.
xi. Employee share and incentive schemes.
xii. Warranty and indemnity insurance and tax risk insurance.

The work is clearly varied and as trainee solicitors we do not usually get to cover each and every aspect of tax law due to the limited time spent in the seat and moving on to the next seat rotation. However, as a qualified solicitor, the various members of the team are able to cover each of the areas above and become specialists in some of the areas.

The work that a trainee solicitor undertakes in a tax department can vary. From discrete pieces of research to larger, on-going matters, such as; assisting with the tax aspects of a corporate transaction, dealing with post-completion matters, or advising clients directly on tax issues that may arise in their course of business (such as VAT returns and obtaining certain reliefs). The seat is quite research-heavy in its advisory practice as opposed to the other three seats I have covered, which were transactional by their nature. The research tasks are generally interesting, and the resources the trainee solicitors use will become very familiar after the first few weeks. If there is an aspect of tax law that the trainee solicitor is interested in, it is also possible to discuss this with the relevant partners. They would then be able to include the trainee solicitor in the relevant deals.

In terms of corporate-related work, trainee solicitors are often asked to help with the tax matters arising out of a transaction. This could involve reviewing the tax documents contained in a data room, or doing some research on a point of law in connection with the deal. Trainee solicitors are also asked to assist with the drafting of the tax deed, the tax warranties, or with Stamp Duty matters post-completion of a transaction. There is a lot of correspondence with HMRC that deals with various other applications for adjudication, including but not limited to group relief applications or adjudications that no stamp duty is payable due to the nature of the parties involved in the transaction.

As research is clearly a large part of a tax trainee solicitors' workload and associates often heavily rely on the trainee solicitors' findings, it is very important that we are thorough and check all available resources - effective research skills are very valuable in this department.

While I have just started the tax seat a month ago, I have already had a good variety of assignments from the team. Even though the team is advisory/transactional, I am already involved with a couple of high-profile investigations by HMRC. This has to be the most interesting experience as it allows me to study the correspondence and structuring that we have undertaken for a client years ago and see the full transaction. It then rests with us as advisers to gather all the relevant information and provide it to HMRC to prove that their reading of the facts against the legal provisions is not sufficient.

While not purely litigation (and it would not count towards my litigation experience as part of my training contract), it is a highly contentious case. Being able to assist the supervising associates in the team with various research and technical analysis is very rewarding. Needless to say, reading the provisions in the statutes and analysing them in detail is a welcome change in my training contract, as it allows me to go back to my roots while studying law at a university.

After having three predominantly (if not purely) transactional seats, I wanted to experience something different while staying true to my interest in corporate law and the corporate department itself. Trainee solicitors in a tax team do not take care of a documents list or conditions precedent checklists on a daily basis, nor do we run transactions or get involved in larger signings. As mentioned above, strong research skills are a must.

Moreover, if you want to succeed in the tax team and impress the supervising associates, you have to be very thorough when reading the law and be open to various interpretations. It is important that you foresee any issues that may arise from your reading of the law and then apply the law to the specific client's circumstances. As I have seen multiple times, there is an infinite number of possibilities how a company group can be structured and even the slightest difference may mean huge changes in the tax treatment of the transaction at hand. As long as the trainee solicitors are thorough, have a natural attention to detail, and are keen to learn on a daily basis, they will surely become a valued member of the team.

One of the best first seats that new trainee solicitors can get is definitely Corporate Transactions (or an equivalent), as it gives you a broad overview of the various fields/sectors and prepares you very well for the rest of your training contract. I have only positive experiences from the department.

It was in this first seat where I experienced probably the biggest deal (in terms of the required documents and structuring steps) for years to come. As trainee solicitors in a purely transactional seat, we are mostly involved with transaction management, document lists and drafting of ancillaries. This deal involved advising the sellers on a sale of a group of companies but since the corporate group was large and the buyer only wanted specific entities, we had to prepare all the documents for a de-merger. The actual completion of the sale then involved the buyer acquiring the holding company under which we have placed all the relevant subsidiaries.

In order to do so, we had well over twenty steps in the structuring paper, many of which had further sub-steps - the documents list was around 150 pages in itself. As a trainee solicitor, in order to be a valued member of the team and help the supervising associates, you have to know the documents and steps almost by heart, especially coming to the completion of the reorganisation."

## Funds at Akin Gump Strauss Hauer & Feld with Associate Melissa Kinsmore-Ward

### About Melissa's Experience:

"I went to a local state primary and high school in my little town, and then onto a separate sixth form in a slightly bigger town. I studied A Levels in Law, Sociology, Business Studies, Maths and Critical Thinking.

I completed my LLB law degree at Warwick University, graduating in 2011. I was very lucky to be graduating with a training contract at Simmons & Simmons LLP as it was a tough few years after the financial crisis of 2008 and a number of my friends were unfortunately not able to obtain a training contract. I completed vacation schemes at a couple of firms in the summer following my second year (2010) and was not entirely taken with those firms based on my experience.

I had not completed a vacation scheme at Simmons & Simmons, so my application was a straight training contract application and I was lucky enough to receive an offer – Simmons & Simmons of course has a great reputation, and all the people I met were lovely, but the main thing that drew me to them, and the reason I accepted their training contract offer, was that on the tour everyone that worked there seemed genuinely happy and lots of people had flowers on their desk, so it seemed like a good environment to work in.

Once graduated, I attended BPP Law School to obtain my LPC (sponsored by Simmons with a grant) and then completed an MBA (legal services) at BPP Business School (which was a Simmons & Simmons sponsored programme with a grant for a year), before starting my training contract in September 2013. The MBA was a great experience as I was able to meet some of the other trainee solicitors in my intake, and I feel like I genuinely learned a lot that I have since used in my career.

It was also helpful because we were placed with some of Simmons & Simmons' clients for our final projects. I was placed with Morgan Stanley and following completion of my project, I was asked to return for a few weeks over the summer as a consultant to broaden my research for them.

During my training contract I undertook seats in IP, a client secondment to Barclays, a seat in funds and an international secondment for corporate in Tokyo. The training at Simmons was generally excellent - I was very fortunate to get all four of my first choice of seats and had great supervisors throughout. The training is well developed, and the processes involved (i.e. seat choice and qualification) run fairly smoothly.

I left Simmons & Simmons in May 2019 and joined Akin Gump's funds team in June 2019 where I currently work. This was the right move for my career and I have no regrets whatsoever as I feel that I have continued to develop at Akin Gump. As of March 2020, I also became a trainee solicitor supervisor which has been challenging given the current environment and everyone working from home, but immensely rewarding.

**The Funds seat at Akin Gump Strauss Hauer & Feld:**

Being a funds lawyer inherently includes a lot of variety in the work that we do. There are days where I do a bit of employment law, financial regulation and litigation, as well as the day-to-day corporate work. Which means you have to have a broad knowledge base (and the confidence to tell clients that you will come back to them if you do not know the answer).

In terms of the types of work I do on a day-to-day basis, I draft and review fund documentation and agreements, I attend board meetings and project calls, I draft proposals for new clients, I negotiate side letters with our client's investors and much more! I also do a lot of project management as that tends to be the key role of the funds lawyer. There is a huge amount of work that we can get involved with and a lot will depend on what the markets are doing, and which partners you gravitate towards as well as what their niche might be.

I am also lucky that Akin Gump appreciates Pro Bono work and client development so I endeavour to do as much Pro Bono and client development as I can fit in. For trainee solicitors considering qualifying into funds, my advice would be that I know that it feels like the be-all-and-end-all to receive a qualification offer from the place you trained - I know I felt that way. However, there are several firms (particularly US firms) that do not have trainee solicitors and are therefore looking for newly qualified solicitors in a variety of areas, so the likelihood is that you will get a job offer somewhere.

Further, unless you have to, try not to accept a job in a practice area that you are not as keen on, just because you want to stay at your firm - people within departments change, but once you pick a practice area, except for the odd occasion when there might be limited scope to change, generally, that is the practice area you will be in for a number of years (possibly your entire career); so pick something that you have a genuine interest in and can see yourself building your career within."

## Working as a Knowledge Lawyer

One career at commercial law firms that I found less explained to me was the path of a knowledge lawyer overseas. Conrad Flaczyk breaks down his journey into law and the experience of becoming a Knowledge Lawyer at Norton Rose Fulbright in Canada:

"The long and winding road of qualifying as a lawyer in Canada is rewarded - at least in part - by a collegial bar, strong rule of law, and world class transactions in major Canadian cities. There are, of course, notable challenges and 'works-in-progress' in the Canadian legal profession, namely, access to justice, diversity, and the availability of entry-level opportunities for law students and recent graduates.

Qualifying as a lawyer in Canada typically requires: (i) completing a four-year undergraduate degree (in any discipline); (ii) sitting the LSAT; (iii) completing three to four years of law school; (iv) passing a licensing exam; and (v) completing an 'Articling' term of roughly ten months with a lawyer or law firm. All in all, becoming qualified as a lawyer in Canada can take eight or more years. A significant commitment.

Canada's legal system is unique in that predominantly English-speaking provinces are governed by common law, while Quebec - Canada's predominantly French-speaking province - is governed by civil law (even though Canada's highest court, the Supreme Court, hears cases from both legal systems). To practice as a lawyer, you need to obtain a license in a particular province (just like a U.S. lawyer must obtain a license to practice in a particular state), and lawyers can become licensed in multiple provinces.

Prior to the pandemic, Canada's legal market was relatively 'hot' and law firms were posting strong numbers for 2018 and 2019 in terms of hiring, revenues, and matter generation. That said, finding an entry-level articling or associate position can be challenging, and there is certainly no guarantee of finding an articling position or a high paying job after law school. Though, law societies have put in place certain substitutes for articling in the form of experiential training courses to prepare law graduates and to allow them to proceed with the licensing process despite any difficulties in securing an articling position.

In the same way that an in-house lawyer serves a company rather than clients, law firms may have lawyers that serve the firm - as a business entity - rather than clients. Knowledge and Innovation departments are two examples of such roles, although there are many others like Compliance lawyers, Conflicts and Ethics lawyers, Hiring and Recruitment lawyers, and certain C-Suite positions like Strategy Officers and Operating Officers. For these kinds of lawyers, the law firm - and its lawyers - are the clients.

Knowledge and Innovation are two distinct departments at Norton Rose Fulbright, although they work closely together. In terms of Knowledge, it is extremely important for law firms to be among the first to know about breaking legal updates from courts, Parliament, and government. Being the first to know is key for many reasons - not the least of which is to provide exceptional client service.

Being the first to know means that lawyers can inform clients of breaking legal updates that affect their business and allowing them to respond to potential risks in a proactive rather than reactive manner (making sure that risks do not escalate to the point of litigation, damage to their brand, or a host of other business risks).

Being the first to know is also a major competitive advantage and useful for matter generation because larger clients - especially those that employ several law firms - retain firms that spot these new risks.

As a Knowledge Lawyer, part of my job, therefore, is to track legislative, case law, and government updates in real time, keeping our lawyers informed, and drafting clients documents to easily explain those updates.

Just like Knowledge lawyers help firms provide exceptional client service and generate new work, so, too, do Innovation lawyers. This department works with clients to learn everything there is to know about their internal legal affairs (how they are organised and, in particular, their time and cost inefficiencies) to develop software-based solutions for making those processes more efficient. Innovation departments employ lawyers who are familiar with and passionate for technology, as well as in-house software engineers who assist with the development of certain software products. Innovation departments are also responsible for innovating internally within the law firm by researching and implementing new tools for making the law firm more efficient, less costly for clients, and improving internal workflows. In these ways, both Knowledge and Innovation departments help keep law firm's competitive vis-a-vis other firms by allowing them to go 'above and beyond' for clients and helping to generate new matters."

## Working as a Technology, Media and Telecommunications (TMT) Lawyer

With clients looking for more for less from their professional service provider, the role of technology has and will continue to play a significant role in the service provided by law firms. This next section looks at the life of a technology lawyer from the perspective of the Global Head of Technology at Pinsent Masons. Simon Colvin shares his insight having pursued a career as a TMT lawyer and the role of technology in the legal sector:

### Simon's Journey:

"I was doing a non-law degree and it was halfway through I was like maybe I am focusing in on the wrong area and the more I thought about it the more business law interested me. The logical approach of how you went through analysis made sense to me and I really enjoyed how you go through case law and how it evolved. It was towards the end of the three-year non-law degree that made me think now I need to shift into something slightly different, which is why I decided to take the conversion.

My interest in technology evolved. When I was a kid if I was given a toy the first thing I would do is take it apart and figure out how it all worked. The true son of an engineer! So, I took that engineering interest that is constantly changing and evolving and applied that dynamic to law. I wanted to similarly go into an area of law where there was always something new happening and that was constantly evolving. So, my childhood and these experiences inspired me to explore the technology space, and that is what gave rise to my career.

**Simon's Role:**

I have quite a number of different roles. I head up the Technology Media and Telecoms team. But also, a lot of the partner role is to run the team and help the team develop and move on so there is an element of my job that is spent on working in a big team. That is why the work we aim to work on is major project work because the team is able to work well together on some really challenging things. As I have moved on in my career my role has changed and being in charge of helping the development of others in the team is a really enjoyable and exciting thing, so I am lucky in that I have different focuses to spend time on.

**The most interesting case:**

Quite some time ago we did a job in the defence sector and it was interesting because it was a big renegotiation with a very strong opposition. The opposition had a regimented approach to how they wanted to do the deal. It was quite interesting because at first, we felt our client did not have much leverage and over time we managed to get the opposition to adapt to a whole different style of running the transaction. It was quite a complicated technology deal but interestingly enough it was grounding. Like a lot of these really big technology deals we were working long hours working side by side with the clients. And, we would go where the client needed us to be.

Working off-site, at one point we were accommodated in an out of season holiday camp which was being rented out. But at another point in time, the client asked us to go to the United States to cover some of the negotiations. So, we upped and went to stay in a hotel there to get the deal done. It showed me that you never know how the deal or transaction will take shape - and the relationship we built with that client was so strong because we were in the room with them day in day out, weeks, months on end and spending all our time with them. It was a great thing to do.

**Career highlights:**

One of the things we do to raise our profile as a firm is to put ourselves forward for awards. One of the amazing highlights for me was a few years ago when we in the TMT team put ourselves forward for an award for a particular deal. A number of other groups in the firm put themselves forward and we went along. You just never know if your deal is even going to be up there once the judges look through the shortlisted deals. TMT was in the back of the brochure, and I expected it would be the last to be announced, but they decided to flip it so that we were the first up. We ended up winning that award first up and so we were absolutely delighted.

Our deal was on a robotics case we worked on and as we approached the judges to receive the award they said that they loved reading about the case. As we sat down there were three other teams on the table from Pinsent Masons all up for awards and we successfully won every single one. The table was just on Cloud Nine. Our senior partner had to be at another event that night so could not attend, but he was looking at the social media feed coming through about us winning all these awards. He was tweeting that he could feel the excitement as Pinsent Masons won awards one after the other. It was just great to be on a table with colleagues who were so excited and were recognised for their hard work.

**What makes a successful technology lawyer:**

Without a doubt you have got to have an interest in technology and it needs to give you a buzz. If technology gives you a buzz and you enjoy watching how it moves on, then you are going to be a better lawyer in that field. Some aspects of being a tech lawyer revolve around commercial - managing the deals and putting in place contracts for supply, build or development of the tech.

Being a commercial lawyer is important but once you are interested you are more likely to research around and get to know the wider space (including all the acronyms). So, the more interested and keener you are the more you are going to add value to the client – you are not just turning up at work as a lawyer to write the contract, but you are interested in what does the solution do and how does that work. It is that sort of background interest that is going to make the lawyer a better fit from the client's perspective too.

I would also say people, people, people. A lot of being a lawyer is about the art of persuasion and providing confidence to a client. So, in an external law firm having those sort of people skills and the emotional intelligence to be on a level with your client and team members is important.

Your knowledge of the law is a given once you are here and enter the door but how you develop relationships internally with clients and how you second guess where a client sees a challenge comes from emotional intelligence and people skills. Which is why I think this is paramount if you are going to make a success of it.

**Future of technology at law firms:**

Super important and it already is. Ten years ago, if you said to me we will have a group of thirty or more software developers sitting in our business as employees I would have laughed and said forget it we are a law firm. But now that is exactly where we are because they are developing bespoke solutions. We are doing two things - we are driving out internal efficiency of what we are doing as lawyers through, for example, the use of AI in big due diligence matters through the use of third-party platforms which we bespoke for the client's needs.

The second is that we are also sitting down with them and our clients to see where the problems and inefficiencies are in their business, particularly in-house legal departments, to ensure we are maximising their potential. So, it is there already, and that will continue to have an exponential effect in the way we do business as a professional services firm with law at our core, and it is great that Pinsent Masons have embraced it so strongly and is leading as a really innovative professional services firm. There are lots of firms that are snapping at our heels with the use of technology, but if you do not invest in that space then it is truly at your peril.

A law firm is a data-rich business - we manage all a vast amount of construction disputes for example. From the number of disputes, we see why things go wrong, if we can draw out the analytics to say what are the trends and how can we help clients prevent those things going wrong in the future, that is of significant value to the clients. We are on a journey on how we capture data. We used to fill in forms to do post analysis; however now we are filling in online data capture tools to build our rich data bank. We need to be constantly doing that to ensure we benefit the most from that data multiplicity we have in our business. It is going to be critical for us to help clients strategically help them spot the trends to manage risk and achieve success in their business.

**Technology - the use of smart contracts:**

This is an interesting topic. There has been a lot of chat about Smart Contracts for a long time, we have not seen mass adoption yet so there is some real value in the approach and certainly in the use of technology and AI in terms of greater efficiency and accuracy. However, many of our clients are not yet ready to embrace that level of automation just yet but we need to wait to see how confidence increases. When confidence increases, then adoption will doubtlessly become far more widespread."

**Technology - the future for lawyers:**

Matthew Wilson, Associate General Counsel, EMEA & APAC at Uber comments:

"I do not think the role of most lawyers will change a ton in the next five years. There are some elements of the job that are being increasingly automated. For instance, low-level contracts, due diligence in M&A transactions and discovery work in litigation leverage technology more and more and that trajectory is likely to continue. However, when it comes to things like negotiation and regulatory engagement we are still a long way away because a lot of the work of lawyers in this space is bespoke. For instance, when it comes to litigation, I do not think the way lawyers need to construct strategy/arguments will not change a ton in the next five years.

The uses of blockchain technologies will become increasingly relevant in things like real estate transactions and purchases of tangible property and assets. Probably a little less so when it comes to buying and selling companies. I personally think this road to using technology started with spell checking functionality during proofreading exercises and document review! What I worry about though is some of that more basic work is how you build rigour into how you train young lawyers. My concern is not constructing bundles and proofreading contracts as we could probably use technology to step in to replace trainee solicitors doing such tasks.

However, these exercises force trainee solicitors to have attention to detail more ingrained early in their careers which is useful. For example, I would have been worse off if I was not reviewing and drafting contracts and really having the time to learn by doing, and understanding the interplay and crossover between things like liability regimes and contracts, warranties, representations, conditions and entire agreement clauses. The big question for me is if trainee solicitors no longer does that work anymore (i.e. if contracts are all automated and not negotiated) then how do we effectively train our junior lawyers?"

## TMT and Pensions at Pinsent Masons with Associate Benjamin Roach

**About Benjamin:**

"I first gave some real thought about what I wanted to do during my A-Levels. I was really interested in business studies and the commercial aspects of other subjects such as DT. I knew that I did not want to go to university to study business and concluded that the things I was really interested in were the regulatory side and the rules. In fact, it was my business studies teacher who suggested a career in law.

In my opinion, the main role of a corporate lawyer is to help businesses succeed within the bounds of the law and to stay on the right side of the law. In TMT for me, there are two sides of it. There is the transactional side - negotiating contracts for technological transactions such as software licence agreements and large-scale technological transformations and IT agreements. At Pinsent Masons, we predominantly act for customers in those agreements, so our job is to make sure that the customers' requirements are captured in the agreement and that it has all the mechanisms in case things go wrong, so the customer is sufficiently protected.

On the flip side there is the advisory side. For instance, a public sector client asked for some advice for applicability of regulations relating to the accessibility of websites in terms of individuals' disability and making sure the website is accessible to those people. The regulation is quite vague and ambiguous, so I was asked to give my view. We prepared a short note of advice for the client. On the advice part - the TMT team at Pinsent Masons has a strong focus on Financial Services. Given the large amount of FS regulation, our job involves advising our clients on the interpretation and implementation of that regulation. For example, this includes giving advice on the open banking rules and financial services outsourcing rules.

**The Pensions seat at Pinsent Masons:**

My pension seat was really varied. It involved more contracts than I had originally expected. Pension schemes are contracts at the end of the day, and you need to have a written document to back up the scheme and set the rules. So, this involved drafting pensions schemes, preparing amendments, and advising on what the rules say and their interpretation. It depends who you act for as there are two parties/sides to a pension scheme - the company who offers the pension scheme and the trustees of the scheme. The scheme documents can be hundreds of pages long so both sides often need advice on what the rules say. That is the contractual side of it, but there is the regulatory side.

Pensions law is possibly one of the most complicated of the different departments that I did a seat in. Mainly because of how regulated it is - Parliament wants to ensure that pensions are protected. So, advising on the complexities of the law and how it impacts a pension scheme was a challenging part. During this seat, we often interacted with barristers on the complex areas. There is added complexity because the rules change so often - there is often a new pension law every two years, if not more regular than that. Most of our clients in pensions were the trustees of the scheme (so the people that are set up to manage the scheme). One of the biggest pension clients I did work for was Cadbury's, where we advised the trustees for the pension fund. Given what had gone on at the company before my seat (having been bought by Kraft Foods), there were multiple pension schemes that could be consolidated. There were other household names we advised, such as GKN Aerospace who are based around Birmingham.

As a Pensions lawyer, you need to be really detailed orientated and be able to read some quite complex legislation and understand it quickly. So, for pensions you need to be quite a strong technical lawyer.

**The transition from Trainee Solicitor to Newly Qualified Solicitor:**

I have always had an interest in technology. It was also a good job that I enjoyed contract law at university because quite a lot of what I do on a daily basis is contracts. In every seat that I did I made sure I got relevant experience as much as possible, so that when it came to qualification, I was able to talk about how my experiences in each seat would make me a good TMT lawyer. Particularly when it came to my commercial seat, I endeavoured to make sure that the contracts that I did had a technology focus, so that when it came to the interview for TMT, I had something to talk about. But even doing a commercial seat reaffirmed to me that doing the technology work would be something that I wanted to do.

My responsibilities did change more than I thought they would when I transitioned from trainee solicitor to newly qualified solicitor. This might have been because I never worked with the TMT team before, but it was more of a transition and a steeper learning curve than expected. I felt that overnight the way you are seen by clients and your peers changes as the word trainee solicitor is dropped before the word solicitor in your title. I felt that people expected you to know everything when the training wheels came off, and you are a qualified lawyer.

However, saying that, my line manager and everyone at the firm was, and is, supportive if I have any questions. As you spend more time as a qualified lawyer, you become more confident and you get to know when you need to ask for help, and that only comes with practice. It is a case of building up your knowledge and knowing when to ask for help. The other key takeaway that I think is important to remember is that clients do not expect you to instantly have the answer, so there is no reason why you cannot tell a client that you need to go away and do a bit of research and discuss it with your team.

**Life at Pinsent Masons and career highlights:**

I have some tips I would offer for trainee solicitors. When I was a final seat trainee solicitor, having not spent any time in the TMT team, I made sure I was reaching out to members of the team for catch-ups and to make sure they were aware that I was applying for the job! Finding out how the team was doing and the work it was doing was really important too, to show that you are on top of that. Other than that, it is essential to prepare for the typical competency-based interview questions.

What I have enjoyed most about Pinsent Masons has always been how friendly and open people are. I have got friends in other law firms who are quite envious about the culture, and how well people get on so the social side is important to me. For instance, a group of us in the TMT team cycled to Paris together over a weekend to raise money for the firm's charity. I think as a firm it is not a daunting place to work and instead is a friendly place to work which cares about making sure you have a life outside of work. There will be times you have to work late, but the partners respect that where they can.

One work and non-work-related career highlight. The non-work-related thing was that as a trainee solicitor, you are really encouraged to get involved in other areas of the firm life, whether that is charity fundraising or organising social events for the office. When I was in Birmingham as a trainee solicitor I got stuck into that and was involved in the social committee and organised the office annual quiz and party. Seeing those come to life and work out was exciting and a bit different from the day job - and allowed me to meet lots of other people. In the Birmingham office of over four hundred people, it puts your name out there – particularly the Christmas party, which was a great opportunity to meet some senior members of the team early on in my career.

Work-related, my career highlight was being sent on client secondment upon qualification. After being a month qualified, I was sent on secondment to Aviva to their digital and data protection team. That was quite a highlight because they were a new team and I developed a really strong relationship with their team so that when I came back to Pinsent Masons, I was the go-to person for liaising with the team because of the relationship I had built with them. I was responsible for advising on data protection aspects of new digital products and services that they were offering.

It was really interesting to see Aviva, a traditional insurer, offering new products and services in a different/digital way. For example, they wanted to make use of Telematics devices in cars, where they could monitor and analyse the ability of the driver and when they drove so as to offer a better price. As a lawyer advising on this matter, I was responsible for advising on the data protection aspects of that because of the significant amounts of personal data collected on customers – such as where drivers were located, what time they often drive, and how well they drive. I was also advising them on the terms and conditions that needed to apply to those policies for the collection of that data in the use of that technology, and their contracts with third-party suppliers who powered the service.

Another big project I worked on was when Pinsent Masons advised Tesco on rolling checkout-less stores. Like all supermarkets, Tesco were looking to roll out a system where you can walk out with items without having to check out, with the customer being charged automatically.

They have invested in a company who owns the technology that allows for this to take place. Our corporate team advised on the corporate transaction, while in TMT we helped negotiate the commercial agreement to enable the trial of the software. The nature of the technology was interesting and quite cutting edge.

The best part of the job is working on projects which are cutting edge – I am interested in how the work will have a significant impact on society. Tesco, for example, is the kind of work that is really going to make an impact. The high-profile nature of the work makes interesting.

**Skills required as a TMT lawyer:**

For TMT, one of the key skills is to have an interest and an understanding of technology and how it works. For example, it can be quite hard to negotiate a license agreement for a 'software as a service' technology if you do not understand how the underlying technology works. There is a subtle difference between negotiating an agreement for Amazon Web Services, for example, compared to negotiating a simple supply agreement for goods (such as pens and pencils). If, for example, the goods such as pens do not work correctly, you can likely source an alternative quickly and easily.

However, if you are negotiating something as complicated and important as Amazon cloud storage and your client has migrated its business to the cloud, and it all goes wrong, the client's business could be significantly impacted! So, having that underlying interest and understanding is important for TMT. Given how contract heavy it is in TMT it is also key to have strong communication and negotiation skills as well. I think being personable and willing to pick things up quite quickly is vital as a lawyer, particularly in technology."

The next chapter explores how to make decisions when preparing for qualification. In particular, this looks at sharing the insight of recruiters who have placed a number of different legal professionals and have decades of experience within the industry.

# Chapter 4: Making decisions as a Newly Qualified Solicitor

This chapter looks at how to prepare for qualification. This is achieved by speaking with recruiters with experience placing professionals ranging from newly qualified solicitors to partners. The perspectives of lawyers are also included in this section to showcase what legal professionals might want to consider when approaching qualification. First up, Robert Hanna who is the Founder of Kissoon Carr shares his insight. Kissoon Carr is a legal recruitment company with over twenty years of combined experience and knowledge on the team.

**Making decisions by Robert Hanna at Kissoon Carr:**

**How should Trainee Solicitors decide where to qualify:**

"There are multiple considerations trainee solicitors should make when deciding where to qualify. These include but are not limited to the culture at the firm, the workload, the type of work, the international nature of the work and the full remuneration package. Thus, to get this information and more, it is vitally important that trainee solicitors research the firms and be as well informed as possible.

The obvious ways to do this are to conduct Google searches, look through the law firm's social media channels, read relevant legal articles and press publications related to the firm and of course the main law firm's website.

Whilst those are useful starting points which will give a general overview, using a platform such as LinkedIn could prove far more beneficial. Connecting with trainee solicitors, associates, partners and HR professionals at your desired law firm, reaching out to them and messaging/voice noting them. This will give the trainee solicitors a far greater insight than any online source could ever give. Further to this, it will also show a lot about the character of the trainee solicitor who has been proactive and gone searching for answers.

In the spirit of being proactive with further due diligence. Trainee solicitors can also look a review sites such as Glassdoor, to get a sense of previous legal professional's experiences with their chosen firm, to see if there are regular positive or negative themes.

Trainee solicitors can also join relevant legal and wider societies which their desired firms may be involved in or connected with; this will give the opportunity to meet lots of people connected to the firm providing valuable additional points of view to be considered.

In terms of the where and the department a trainee solicitor wishes to qualify, this decision should, in my view, be based on the work that they are doing i.e. what they could see themselves doing on a daily basis for the rest of their careers, and what they enjoy most. I would be reluctant to advise anyone that you should qualify into a department that you have enjoyed most on a personal level or has the best chances of quick progression. People come and go, and structures change. If you choose to qualify into something because a certain colleague was a laugh and the work is okay then you are in for a shock when that person leaves and you are stuck doing work that you are not passionate about.

The corporate culture of the firm must suit you. Similarly, the type of firm and its ability to assist with your own career aspirations is vitally important. I would not pick a firm just because it pays more, that only ends badly in the long run. Rome was not built in a day and trainee solicitors would be well-advised not to simply chase the biggest salary. The bigger salaries will come, particularly if you take care with the decisions you make early on. Choose a firm which aligns with your core values and ensure you go with your gut!

**Specific considerations:**

Searching for a law firm to qualify at throws up many considerations that should be made. As a trainee solicitor it is essential to find a firm that fits your personal style, career aspirations and character. Finding a law firm that shares the same beliefs, work ethos and culture you are looking for is essential as this will allow you as a trainee solicitor to excel and learn as much as possible in the two years of training.

Further to this, when deciding on firms look for places where you get on and have a strong relationship with the senior associates/partners. As a trainee solicitor, you are looking to learn and develop, and this will be a lot easier if you have a strong rapport with the law firms' partners.

Ensure you have done thorough research into a firm. As if you wish to work on complex multi-jurisdictional global matters in one particular area of law, ensure the law firm is currently offering that, or this is on their radar in line with your career timelines. As if they do not, whilst that firm might be a prestigious player in the market for other legal professionals, it would not be right for you. I know many trainee solicitors who have chosen diverse cultures and workload as key considerations over salary. For example, opinions are great, but to stress, go with what is right & important to you!

**What to expect from the Trainee Solicitor to Newly Qualified Solicitor transition:**

It is essential for law firms to equip their trainee solicitors with the right resources and opportunities to help them feel confident upon qualification. However, do not expect a huge change immediately. You leave work on the Friday as a trainee solicitor but arrive on the following Monday as a newly qualified solicitor. There is no immediate difference in your day-to-day responsibilities. Over the course of the first few months, you will find you will be given greater responsibility both in terms of work and as a mentor for new trainee solicitors, but it will be a gradual process.

With the transition to a newly qualified solicitor from a trainee solicitor there will be a greater sense of independence and perhaps a greater sense of expectation from the more senior associates. You can expect higher expectations on the quality of work produced and that you maintain a proactive attitude. With this in mind however, guidance and help can still be expected, and there will be plenty of chances to work with partners and senior associates on cases throughout the year.

**Advice for final seat Trainee Solicitors:**

In terms of advice for final seaters, do not get complacent! That said it is okay for final seaters to feel scared about the next step of their journey, but what is key is to feel confident that you have got the necessary training you need to be able to handle the workload and challenges of newly qualified solicitors. Moreover, even as a newly qualified solicitor, you can still ask questions when you are unsure about something and need guidance.

It would be wise to start thinking about the future and networking with people within the legal sphere. Take nothing for granted, do not assume your firm will have a seat for you upon qualification particularly considering COVID-19. Proactively networking within the firm to build relationships with the associates & partners in the areas you wish to qualify is strongly encouraged to ensure you will be front of mind for when the time is right.

Think about how you can bring additional value to your law firm to go above and beyond your legal daily responsibilities, so the firm sees you as a long-term asset and someone worth keeping on top of your legal technical capabilities. Could you start a meaningful society and/or foster a long-term lucrative client relationship through your own networks? These are just some simple examples to get you thinking of how final seaters can add more value to their law firm to stand out.

Whilst maintaining the high-quality of work in your final seat, a final seater could perhaps interact and engage with legal recruiters and decide on the medium-long term future of their legal career. You may be retained by the firm with which you trained but seeking out new opportunities and networking with legal recruitment consultants, peers and contacts in other firms should also be explored. If your final seat is not one that you are qualifying into, do not just switch off. The department may be a source of work in the future too!

**What advice would you give to Newly Qualified Solicitors:**

The job interview continues permanently - next stops are any or all of associate, senior associate, legal director, partner. As a newly qualified solicitor you would have picked your practice area and will be looking to get as much exposure as possible.

One piece of advice I would give is to find someone who is a lot more senior than yourself, who works in the same practice area, who you get on with on a friendship level and ask them to mentor you. Mentorship is vitally important, but perhaps not often used in the legal sphere, find a mentor and he/she will teach you and guide you as a newly qualified solicitor.

Always remain intellectually curious and embrace legal technology movements. Consistently research and upskill yourself in the legal technology area particularly as this is the future and law firms will be looking for future skill sets as well as traditional legal skill sets. Always network, join societies, attend workshops on career development, feature on podcasts, produce engaging content to build your personal brand, this is vitally important as an aspiring lawyer in the modern world! Be mindful there is an internal market for your work and treat your partners as your clients.

**What advice would you give to Trainee Solicitors looking to move to another firm:**

Trainee solicitors need lots of information on how to go about moving to other firms and what that would mean for their long-term careers. First of all, find out and ask yourself why you wish to move. This is important as you do not want to move to a similar firm and encounter the same problems, also moving from firm to firm is not an attractive thing to have on your CV so take time in researching and understanding why you want to make that move.

Money should not be the sole driving factor whilst it might be tempting having the prospect of almost doubling your salary if you are at a UK firm considering a US law firm. There are many more important factors: client exposure, corporate culture, career progression, ability to get involved with business development, five-year plan, market reputation, and responsibility given to junior lawyers. This is not an exhaustive list but just some of the key things to look for. For example, if you are at a Silver Circle firm does moving to another Silver Circle make sense? Potentially, but it has to offer what you might be missing your current firm and what is important to you!

Research and investigate the new firm's associate retention levels, Well-being programmes on top of the quality and quantity of work and structure of team. You will want to know how you will be targeted and the overall culture and job satisfaction levels, plus why the law firm is looking to hire? Have they lost people, or is this a growth opportunity or is it a rebuild both have positives and negatives to be considered!

You become the 'new person' again. You must start all over again if you are moving at an early stage of your career. This is quite significant and potentially demoralising. Equally, however, you must see it as an opportunity to impress again (or start over if it has gone badly thus far!).

But equally, expect the unexpected! Jobs tend to come to you once you reach one to two years PQE. Recruiters will spam your LinkedIn inboxes weekly. If you are actively searching, then registering with a with one of a select few recruiters will save you a lot of time. In terms of timing, this is on a case by case basis as for some we have supported through Kissoon Carr relatively quickly, but it is probably not unusual for it to take three to six months plus in terms of hunting.

The legal job market is still candidate led, so typically an interview process can take anywhere between four to six weeks, with two to three rounds of interview (some including competency or technical based case study tests) as a guide. With the birth of more video interviewing due to COVID-19, you have an opportunity to speak and meet with more partners and associates during interview processes. Most processes will also offer an informal team meeting towards the end, which helps assess your overall team fit and hopefully cementing your positive gut feeling about the opportunity.

You will typically have a three months' notice period to be mindful of. If you are moving as a one to two years PQE then the interview is probably going to be more technical based and more of an interrogation of your experience to-date. Once you get to three years PQE+ interviews can be less technical but more of a discussion to see if you are a good fit, and you have the potential to bring in work.

Having a good relationship with a legal recruitment consultant can be invaluable and massively beneficial! They will have great relationships with partners and senior associates at a lot of firms that may appeal to you. Further to this, they will know what sort of culture to expect and can relay such information to you as a candidate.

They are your source of up to date market information (i.e. salary insights, bonuses, promotion timelines from one firm to another), trends in the market, knowledge of what competitor firms are doing, ability to offer careers advice, CV advice, interview preparation when necessary. They also act as a trusted advisor, be proactive and provide information tailored to you.

Whilst acting as a sound board, they can be a reality check should you think things might be good or bad versus other firm cultures or hiring. A recruitment consultant is also expected to consult so you should ask them to do that in areas you want more information, as they are in the market day in and day out. They can save you a lot of time. What is also important is that you have a recruitment consultant who (a) believes in you; (b) you can trust; and (c) you get on with. The recruitment consultant may be with you for your entire career if it works out, so it is a precious relationship!

**Advantages and disadvantages of working at different types of firms:**

One person's 'pros' will be another person's 'cons' so there is no one size fits all. We have worked with a range of newly qualified solicitors at a range of firms over the years and things do change!

Some say in larger UK & US firms, you become a small cog in a giant wheel that runs on autopilot. The pay can be better, but the lifestyle may be worse. The top 100 firms might be more challenging still. It is in a saturated market, and the senior-level decision-makers within the firm may resist change. That can be frustrating for junior lawyers.

At the smaller firm, you may be able to stand out, you may be given great responsibility/autonomy, and you will have greater control of your career and direction of travel. Although, the trade-off may be pay, less security, fewer opportunities for progression, fewer resources, more administrative work, and a greater need for it to be a nice place to work/have nice colleagues.

Being a newly qualified solicitor at the different types of law firms throws up many advantages and disadvantages. A newly qualified solicitor at a Magic Circle law firm may be expected to carry out a lot of work independently where help from partners may be scarcer. Further to this, the work-life balance could be more in favour of the work side than the life side. Hours will be long and a free weekend might be hard to come by. However, these disadvantages do not go unnoticed, and Magic Circle firms reflect that in the salary of a newly qualified solicitor which can reach over £100k including a bonus.

Further to this, at a Magic Circle law firm, the quality of the work may be better than a smaller boutique. A boutique firm for a newly qualified solicitor has lots of benefits from a training and closer-knit team standpoint. The number of associates and partners is lower than a Magic

Circle law firm, and therefore the interaction with partners is more frequent. In comparison to a Magic Circle law firm boutique newly qualified solicitors may have a better quality of social life, but as a result, the yearly salary will not be as high.

Yes, top US firms will pay you the most in the market, sometimes double your salary over another UK. However, the question 'should I go to a Silver Circle, Magic Circle, American, Boutique or specialist' is down to what motivates you! The days of training with one law firm and staying there forever have simply gone. There has been a growth of alternative law firm models emerging over recent years such as cloud-based and dispersed based law firms. In addition to legal technology, legal process and design are becoming more and more a part of everyday legal life. Thus, lawyers have lots of choice.

Of course, there is always the in-house option but that is not the only option nowadays. No two large firms are the same - Jones Days have a non-rotational training contract system for example so you have to go out there which they believe fosters an early-stage business development skill set which is good to have for those who wish to be a partner one day. Your legal career is a marathon not a sprint, you will have highs and lows that is the same in any profession, surround yourself by inspirational and positive people and stay hungry to learn!"

**Matthew Wilson, Associate General Counsel, EMEA & APAC at Uber**

In terms of tips to prepare for qualification, "think about what you want the next five years of your career to look like and ask yourself do you actually know what you want to be doing during and at the end of that time? If you do not then try and stay as broad as possible in terms of the seats you do and what you qualify into. We all have choices to make every single day, and one of those is to show up as bright, energetic and enthusiastic as opposed to negative and grumpy. Try not to be an Eeyore!

Remember that when you are going through the qualification process, whatever you choose you are always going to be able to make different choices after and take your career in different directions later if you really want to.

That should be a real comfort when you make decisions about qualification because you are still able to take your career in different directions. Your whole future does not depend on what decision you make at qualification - it is just another step but you can always change direction.

There are some people I trained with at Baker McKenzie who I thought would stay and be partners forever at Bakers, and they are not even lawyers anymore.

They realised that it was not for them which is fine but they decided to make a new move. I did the same when I left. You are always better off doing something that makes you happy and engaged over something that makes you miserable. I loved Bakers and the people there but realised that being in private practice was not for me in the long term - for other people, it is.

I would also really recommend building the muscle that allows you to be open to learning from everyone around you, whether that is incorporating characteristics you find impressive in others or remembering things people do that you think you would approach a different way. You will come across a lot of both and learning from those situations is invaluable.

If you had said to me when I was a trainee solicitor at Baker McKenzie that in fifteen years' time you will be living in Amsterdam, and one of the things you would be doing in 2019 is represent the company you work for in front of the Competition Commission of Pakistan in Islamabad three times in one year, I would have just laughed at you but that is what happened last year!

The company I work for at the moment, Uber, did not even exist fifteen years ago. In a nutshell, through the choices we make we all have a greater ability to determine our future and destiny than we think we do. Not everyone will agree with those choices though, and you will need a decent amount of courage at times!"

### Associate Sakhee Gantra at Mishcon de Reya

"There are a number of factors you should consider when deciding which department you would like to qualify into. Firstly, and most importantly, do you enjoy the type of work? When thinking about this, you should look at the work done by the associates in the department (as ultimately this is the work you will end up doing) and not just the work you did as a trainee solicitor.

Secondly, you should consider the way in which you like to work. For example, some practice areas may have more unpredictable hours whilst others may be steadier. Some practice areas may be purely transactional or advisory or litigious whilst others might have a mix of these.

Thirdly, think about your longer-term goals and objectives and the extent to which the practice area you choose will enable you to achieve these. Finally, whilst this should not be the main reason for your choice, think about the people you will be working with and the culture in the department you are considering.

In terms of preparing for qualification, take some time to carefully consider the factors outlined above. Be honest with yourself and talk to friends and family who know you well and might be able to provide good insights. In addition, talk to as many people as you can in the departments that you are interested in - not only will this help you to make a well-informed decision but it will also ensure you are front of mind when the department is deciding who to hire.

The transition from trainee solicitor to newly qualified solicitor is a fairly big step up. One of the biggest differences I found was that clients do not necessarily know that you are a newly qualified solicitor and therefore there can be greater expectations and a lot more responsibility. It is important to embrace this but also ask for help from others in the department where you need it. It is a challenging shift but also a really exciting one."

**Associate Adam Hattersley at Fieldfisher**

"For me deciding on where to qualify was very much market-driven. At the time I qualified the EU referendum had just taken place so the firms (along with the rest of the country) were a little reluctant to recruit until the impact of the result could be seen. As I had five years of litigation experience by the time I came to qualify, I was convinced I wanted to be a litigator, a property litigator to be more specific.

The only issue was that there were not many firms recruiting in that area at the time.

After a few interviews, I was approached by my recruiter for a role in a completely different area, and more surprisingly, a non-contentious position. I went to the interview and had a really good feeling about the firm and the team. I was lucky as I have really enjoyed my area of law and could not imagine being a litigator now.

It is difficult to decide what area you want to qualify in but my advice in this area is that it is easier as a starting point to work out what areas you do not want to work in. During your training contract, you may have been exposed to certain areas that you really did not enjoy or had no interest in. In these instances, it is easy to rule these out.

It is also one of the only points in your career that you can be selfish. You need to decide which is best for you. My experience was slightly different as there were economic considerations at play, but generally you should push for the role and firm that you want. It can be difficult to change after a few years PQE, so do what is best for you.

This must also be considered alongside being open-minded. Had I have pursued a role in property litigation, there is a good chance I would have wanted to change by now. Had I not been open-minded to my current role, I may have missed out.

I found the transition from being a trainee solicitor to a newly qualified solicitor hard. I had trained at a smaller firm. This meant there was much more focus on billing and bringing in work to the firm. When I moved on qualification, the step-up in terms of position/firm and wage made me feel there were much bigger expectations of me. After a few weeks of taking on too much work and working long hours, my boss approached me and said not to take on too much as I was learning the role and that he was not expecting me to be the finished product. That for me was a huge help as it helped me realise most firms see a newly qualified solicitor as an extension of the training contract.

The biggest change for me was the feeling of losing a safety net slightly. I do not think this was actually the case, but once qualified, there is a feeling of the training wheels coming off. For me, I found the best way to deal with this was to continue to ask questions when I was unsure of anything, as well as to have confidence in my abilities.

A tip for trainee solicitors would be to get yourself organised early! Do not wait for an offer from your firm, it is always best to have a plan B. I think there is often a common misconception that it you interview at other firms or look around in the job market upon approaching qualification, that your current firm will view this negatively or that you are going behind their back.

Firstly, it is prudent to make sure you are secure with a job offer. The worst thing you can do is get close to the qualification date before finding out your firm may not have a vacancy in the area you want to qualify into, leaving you little time to find an alternative. Secondly, the firm may fear the risk of losing you and seek to secure you in advance. It would be foolish not to get yourself prepared for qualification regardless of whether this be at your firm or elsewhere.

The best aspect of being an associate - you are qualified! All that hard work and years of training have paid off. The status and feeling of being a solicitor cannot be underestimated. The worst - you are qualified! Time to stand on your own two feet and start your career. It is often a time of self-doubt and anxiety as I said earlier the safety wheels are now off.

The advice I would give to newly qualified solicitors would be to have faith in your abilities, you are there on merit so always remember that if you start to doubt yourself. You are not the finished article! This is the start of your career, not the end. The firms will expect you to be learning still so do not feel it is a weakness to continue to ask questions. It is often just an extension of your training contract."

Finally, another option that trainee solicitors might consider during the transition to qualification is moving in-house. Daniel Harris, an Associate Director at Robert Walters Legal Recruitment Company, explains the routes into in-house positions. As a well-known outfit based in the city, Daniel and his team have placed a number of newly qualified solicitors into in-house positions. Over to Daniel for his insight!

## **Moving In-house by Daniel Harris at Robert Walters Legal Recruitment Company**

"For many junior lawyers, taking an in-house role, it is becoming a more widely available option. Lawyers at the early stages of their career recognise the benefits of an in-house role and organisations recognise the value in-house lawyers bring as a supplement to (or, in some cases, a replacement of) the legal support traditionally undertaken by private practice firms. In addition, an increasing number and variety of organisations are looking to employ in-house lawyers, from multinational companies to start-ups (as well as the military, local government and NGOs).

A career in-house can be extremely varied, interesting and rewarding. It is different from working in private practice so if you have ever thought about pursuing the in-house route, there are some key considerations to consider and some myths which can be busted.

Put simply, private practice lawyers are income generators. In companies, lawyers are an expensive overhead. So why would a company seek to add to its headcount and cost for a service when the traditional view would be to outsource?

Despite being a cost overhead, an in-house team represents cost efficiency. Companies instruct lawyers in practice when they do not have the necessary expertise in their in-house legal department, or the workload handled by the in-house team becomes unmanageable. Law firm costs are very high, so when the overflow becomes continuing and costs mount, a company may look to expand its team.

In-house roles expose junior lawyers to real responsibility very early. Remember that companies hire almost as a last repost when cost pressure makes a hire irresistible, and companies want an immediate return on the investment. Lawyers are thus expected to get involved in the role right from the start. That is not to say that they should be expected to be thrown completely in at the deep end, and enlightened companies will have clear and defined onboarding programmes allowing for efficient development.

Very large organisations will have specialists but, in the main, junior lawyers in-house can expect to have a generalist role which will mean a varied technical workload. In general, this will mean not specialising too early on in their careers and having a more rounded approach to their legal practice.

In summary, it is often said that private practice lawyers are brought in and out of the projects and work a company does, and that junior lawyers have the full view and context of the role. This can be overstated, but in general in-house lawyers will have a deep understanding of the details of their company's strategy in a way which some practices support lawyers may not."

Having briefly discussed the transition to moving in-house, the next chapter takes a more in-depth look at life working in-house by speaking to various legal professionals who have made this move.

# Chapter 5: Working In-House

Working in-house is a path many lawyers consider at some point in their careers. This chapter looks at exploring the different routes into working in-house. With careers being non-linear, the legal professionals in this section convey the different routes they have taken. The main options looked at include: working as a paralegal, undertaking client secondments, undertaking a training contract in-house or moving in-house from private practice.

**<u>Working at Channel 4</u>**

There is often a gap of knowledge about beginning and ending a training contract in-house. When discovering a career in commercial law, aspiring solicitors are drawn towards the opportunities created by commercial law firms in private practice. However, whilst they are niche, there are still opportunities to secure training contracts in-house. Amelia Wilson draws upon her experience training at Channel 4 and recently qualifying as a solicitor:

"I have always loved television, and I fell into working in it by doing a YTS work placement at a company that managed competitions and votes for TV, radio and publishing. I started as an office junior, sorting faxes and making coffee. I did that for two years and saw an advert for an account executive, I was put off by the fact you needed a degree but I asked about it and was encouraged to apply.

I did not get the first role, but I got the next one that came up and luckily that was looking after GMTV and regional news, which I absolutely loved. I worked my way up to account manager and looked after the whole Channel 5 account - which included the CSI competition- my favourite show at the time.

I had been at the company for six years and was offered a role at Endemol. I decided to take it as I wanted to move away from a supplier role. I loved Endemol, and I still have the pleasure of working with them regularly. My role was made redundant, though and thankfully I was offered a six months temporary contract at Channel 4, thirteen years on I am still there!

My role was originally in new media complying interactive services such as the Big Brother Vote, my job was brought under the Legal and compliance department within a few months and it was around this time I wondered if I could do more to further my education. I looked at doing a finance course but quickly realised at the open day that it was not for me. I then went to Birkbeck and spoke to a wonderful professor there who really inspired me and told me that it did not matter that I did not have A-Levels. He later became my Human Rights professor and I still love to read about his work in this field.

I did my LLB part-time, it took me a while as I had a baby half-way through the course. I finished my LLB and then took a year break before thinking about the LPC. The Channel agreed to support me with this, and I am incredibly grateful for this. I then went on to start my training contract in March 2019.

I really enjoyed my secondment at Reed Smith. I have never worked in private practice and I got so much out of it. I worked for some wonderful partners and one really pushed me to go back to the leading textbooks in the area I was looking at. I spent a lot of time in their library and looking at the leading practitioners. I even took these massive books home and read them on the train and at weekends and became quite a geek!

I also did a seat with the data protection team, which I really enjoyed. It is such a current topic, and it has an impact in so many areas of our lives. I am continually spotting data protection concerns in my everyday life! I would like to continue in media. I love television and I love working with production teams. I am so proud when I see something on TV that I complied. I also enjoy privacy and reputation management; the Johnny Depp/Amber Head trial is the most incredible libel trial I have ever followed but some of the historical cases are also incredibly interesting. I always remember Naomi Campbell versus NGN being one of the first I studied in this area.

Responsibility wise as a lawyer there is no average week in TV! You can either be working on a long-term documentary over a period of months or a very fast turn-around commission, particularly since COVID-19. You have to adapt your skills to work on various genres; serious documentaries require different legal skills and emphasis than the likes of entertainment shows.

I also work with sales on sponsorship and advertising, which I really enjoy, it is incredibly fast paced and demanding, which I thrive on. I did a lot of live programming early in my career and I do like that buzz when I do those shows again. We have incredibly thorough contingency plans, but sometimes shows can throw you a curveball, and you have to think on your feet!"

## Moving from private practice to UBS

For many aspiring and existing solicitors considering a move in-house might be something you would like to explore. Daniel Lo is a Legal Counsel at UBS and shares his journey:

"I fell into private equity by happenstance. When I moved from Canada to Hong Kong, I took up a role as an in-house counsel at a private equity firm because it looked like a good blend of something I had some experience in (M&A and commercial law) and something I was interested in and wanted to learn more about (investment funds). Right away I was attracted to the fast-paced nature of the investment process and was also able to learn about the commercial rationale behind particular investment strategies.

Private equity has also become a popular practice area in Asia so my arrival in Hong Kong worked well. Since then I have continued to build my private equity legal career by moving to Singapore and working within the investment funds and corporate team at Walkers (an international offshore law firm), and most recently joining UBS Asset Management in their investment funds team.

My move from Dentons to my current role at UBS has been a bit of a roller-coaster ride, involving multiple pivots in terms of geography (Canada to Hong Kong to Singapore), practice areas (started with an energy transactions practice to private equity), and work environment (private practice to in-house to private practice and finally back to in-house). There were new challenges behind every pivot that I had made.

When I moved from Dentons in Canada to a private equity firm in Hong Kong, I had to adjust to not just a new country, but also operating in a Chinese-speaking environment and within an in-house company setting. Making the jump from Hong Kong to Singapore also was challenging as it was also a new country, but this time it was adapting back into a law firm setting and also having to learn the laws of two countries that I had no familiarity with (Cayman Islands and the British Virgin Islands). My most recent move has been probably the smoothest transition as I did not have to move to a new country, I am returning back into an in-house role, and am practising in investment funds which is an area that I have been working on for the past three years.

One tip I would give to anyone considering a move is to make sure the in-house role you decide on has a wide variety of work and not too narrow in scope. As a junior lawyer, you want to be exposed to as much as possible so that you can decide how to shape your career later on as you become more senior. Gaining a variety of experiences is also great for if you want to later on jump back into a law firm because you have a lot more to bring to the table.

In terms of responsibilities, my practice revolves around investment funds. I facilitate the launch and ongoing administration of retail investment funds in Singapore through the review of prospectuses, investment management agreements, trust deeds, memorandum and articles of association, and other ancillary documents. I assist with general corporate secretarial duties for our UBS's Singapore based asset manager, such as drafting board resolutions and minutes. Lastly, I advise on regulatory updates to the investment funds space to ensure that UBS's fund products are following local and international laws and regulations.

A career highlight for me so far has to be the journey that I went on to get called to the bar in the British Virgin Islands. My previous firm was an international offshore law firm, so getting called in one of the jurisdictions that I was practising was a requirement. The journey involved four connecting flights (Singapore to London to Miami to Puerto Rico to the BVI) with one hotel break in between this 24-hour madness. Throw in missed flights due to tropical storms and lots of overpriced airport food and you have got yourself a pretty stressful experience.

However, once I arrived in Tortola and soaked in the Caribbean sun and sand, it was all worth it. The bar call took a total of five minutes and was in a makeshift court-room (because the BVI was still recovering from Hurricane Irma), then the day after I began my journey back to Singapore with another four connecting flights. Safe to say, I was thoroughly done with flying for a while.

One example of a case I found interesting was when I worked as legal counsel at the private equity firm in Hong Kong. I was involved with a string of investment transactions that were in the healthcare tech space. I found these investments exciting to be a part of because I was able to gain exposure into an area that was very hot at the time, and I was also able to see behind the curtain into which other investors were going in on these same companies. Strategically for the firm, I was also able to understand their investment strategy more clearly, which helped me become more commercially conscious in my role as legal counsel.

In my opinion, developing a 'gritty' mindset during my junior years has helped me thrive now. Being able to push through difficult situations and coming out stronger is something that I practice, sometimes putting myself in these situations willingly.

Always being open to learn new things, has allowed me gain so much exposure into different practice areas, and also with non-law related topics that will benefit me as a lawyer, such as picking up personal branding and marketing knowledge.

My most interesting non-law experience was when I ran a student painting franchise back in university in Canada for two years. For those two years, each season meant something different for me. Autumn season meant preparing my business plan and setting ambitious sales and production goals so I can break even and hopefully save enough to pay tuition. Winter season meant going door to door in -25 degrees every day after class to book summer painting projects.

Spring season meant hiring and training a team of twenty students to paint windows/doors/garages/decks, and ramping up sales bookings as competing student painting companies rolled in. Summer season meant ninety hours a week of painting (rain or shine), non-stop sales calls, staff turnover, dealing with upset customers, re-evaluating business plans. Although I was exhausted beyond belief, the thrill of owning my own business taught me two valuable things that I carry into my career as a lawyer you need to take initiative otherwise nothing will happen, and never be outhustled."

**Moving from BBC to private practice**

Having just shared the insight of Daniel Lo who moved from private practice to in-house, I thought it would be important to share the insight of a lawyer who did the opposite. Benjamin Roach, a TMT Associate at Pinsent Masons, shares his insight into working at the Future Media Division at the BBC before moving to Pinsent Masons:

"From a day to day perspective I was negotiating contracts with BBC partners for either trials of new services, or to get BBC services onto partner devices. One of the trial services we did was for a VR company called Oculus Rift, which are now owned by Facebook now. It was for creating some example programmes in virtual reality format. You could put the virtual headset on the Oculus Rift and walk around a studio. We did a David Attenborough trial where you could watch the show using a VR headset to get a 360 look around. The more day to day work was to get BBC iPlayer, BBC news and sport onto connected TV's, mobile phones and other devices.

Given how closely we worked with partners, they would come to us with pre-release versions of devices or services and ask for our help to get BBC services onto the device/service prior to launch. The other main area of work was doing carriage agreements with Sky and Virgin to get the BBC channels onto their platforms. It was all negotiating contracts to take instructions and working out what was important for them and making sure the contract reflected that. As a more junior member of the team, I was also responsible for managing the signed contracts and ensuring the contracts were stored and logged properly.

The transition in-house to private practice was a bit strange. There was a year gap between me leaving the BBC and going to Pinsent Masons to begin my training contract. In that year I did my LPC. That gap was quite jarring, but the in-house role was quite a good stepping-stone. Working in-house made me appreciate what makes a good private practice lawyer and what does not. It teaches you about what in-house lawyers' value and appreciate from private practice lawyers in terms of how advice is presented and prepared.

You could ask the same question to different law firms and some would give you a fifteen-page report whereas others would give you a direct response to what you needed. I learnt what my internal client cared about and what an internal lawyer found useful in terms of presenting advice clearly and concisely. It sounds silly and perhaps obvious, but not sitting on the fence is really important. A lot of private practice lawyers would provide advice which 'could be this or could be that' on topics that really, they should have come to a view on. So, it was a really useful experience to make the transition easily."

## Working at Euro Car Parts Limited

In this section we hear from Jahed Hussain who works as a Legal Counsel at Euro Car Parts Limited:

"My average week consists of dealing with a handful of commercial contracts, long-term projects and business as usual work such as dealing with GDPR queries, intellectual property and supporting Senior Legal Counsel with disputes. I have to liaise with more than a dozen stakeholders in any given week and the majority of my week is occupied by meetings to discuss new projects, existing issues and the client's long-term business requirements.

I primarily do commercially focused work and have been involved in distribution agreements, terms and conditions of purchase and sale, SaaS agreements, turnkey agreements, NDAs, rebate agreements and cross-border/pan-European agreements relating to the supply of goods.

The best aspects of the work would be the diversity and exposure that I have obtained, which is making me a well-rounded in-house lawyer. I have also been given the autonomy to take the lead of projects and gain valuable experience. A challenging aspect would be having conflicting deadlines and not always receiving detailed, clear instructions from clients on the requirements which could potentially cause delays.

Working in-house suits the type of person who is willing to think beyond the legal requirements and focus on the client's business requirements. This means that you have to be willing to listen and be patient in order to obtain key information from the client. It requires someone who is approachable and can maintain effective relationships.

In terms of deciding where to qualify, I worked as a paralegal in both private practice and in-house which allowed me to weigh up my options and understand my personality. This allowed me to make an informed choice that I wanted to pursue a career in-house.

The experience of training in-house has been substantially developed, and my understanding of businesses and what actually happens within companies. I now appreciate that being a lawyer is not just about drafting a legal report or finalising a contract, but it is about understanding the impact that the client is looking to make and how best you can help the client achieve that. I was fortunate to have fantastic mentors/supervisors in my team who have decades of experience. This has been a steep learning curve but I am slowly seeing the rewards as a professional.

This experience significantly differs from my private practice peers. In particular, I have been given more autonomy, responsibility, accountability and trust when it comes to negotiating for and on behalf of the client. My understanding of commercial law appears to be more robust than a lot of my friends who are trainee solicitors doing a commercial seat. I would highly recommend that every trainee solicitor applies for a secondment where possible.

My favourite aspect has been the direct client contact and the opportunity to see the end result of the legal work that I do. The worst aspect would probably be not having peers/other Trainee solicitors to share ideas with due to the size of the team.

As an in-house trainee solicitor my client is also my employer. This makes it easier to develop internal networks and maintain effective relationships. You have to be aware of clashing personalities in-house and need to have the resilience and capability to adapt to different stakeholders whilst also staying independent. I develop my external networks by attending networking events and doing extensive mentoring to support future solicitors. I find this to be an effective way to make a real difference to the legal profession which is lacking in diversity (ethnic, religious, status). I think it is important for every young lawyer of this generation to find a positive way to support the changing landscape and stand up for what is right instead of going with the status quo."

## Undertaking a client secondment with Barclays during a training contract

During a training contract, you might get the opportunity to go and work for a client of the firm. This is a great opportunity to experience working in-house and familiarise yourself with the day to day challenges the business overcomes. Melissa Kinsmore-Ward shares her insight of undertaking a client secondment at Barclays:

"This was an eye-opening experience – I was very lucky to be in a relatively small team in Barclays and was therefore given a lot of responsibility which was a great learning experience.

I was sat within the risk solutions group which mainly dealt with hedging and derivatives agreements – therefore, most of my work was reviewing agreements and amending in line with the bank's policy regarding what they were willing and unwilling to accept within certain parameters for each of their clients. I was also on call for the business team when they had questions or last-minute requirements, so we worked with them closely either on calls or in meetings.

The best aspect was really getting to understand what the in-house legal team experienced. As external counsel, we do not face the same pressures from the business as often we are dealing with a GC within our client's organisation; however, when you are in-house legal counsel, you are dealing with the 'front line' and having to answer quick fire questions in a clear way, all whilst being considered a cost centre because you do not technically make any money for the business (though one could argue you save the business a lot of money in potential legal actions and regulatory fines). It was also invaluable in learning how to communicate with non-lawyers. As mentioned, in most departments, the client you will be speaking with will be a lawyer, and therefore it is easy to fall into speaking with legal terminology.

However, on secondment, you are dealing with business people that do not have law degrees. You therefore need to learn quickly how to provide advice in a clear and easily understood way. Further, you appreciate very quickly (after receiving advice from external counsel that is ten pages long with lots of caveats and no clear outcome), that you need to, where possible, provide 'yes'/'no' advice to the business, because essentially they want to know if they can or cannot do something, and it is in-house counsel's role to say either 'yes, you can' or 'no, you cannot'.

Finally, you have to have a good understanding of the underlying product because the business people will assume you know the product and therefore the legal implications, so if you do not understand the underlying product, it is useful and important to ask for an explanation so you could prepare appropriate advice.

The worst aspect which I have alluded to above is that in-house legal teams are considered a cost centre in most organisations due to the fact that you do not actually bring in any revenue (much like IT and HR). This means that there is constantly a push to reduce costs, and I was unfortunately on secondment when rounds of redundancies were announced, which was a low point.

Tips for this seat would be to learn as much about the underlying products as you can before starting, and network as much as possible whilst you are there with people of a similar level to you as they may well become the GC in years to come (of that client or a different client) and it is a great opportunity to start building your network."

## **Working at Howlett Brown Limited**

Laura Durrant shares her journey into law and insight as ex Head of Litigation, Regulatory and Investigations at RBS. Laura also trained and qualified at Herbert Smith Freehills and was a partner at White & Case before becoming Director of Howlett Brown Limited and Director of Associo Limited in 2019:

"I managed to get some unpaid work experience as a teenager in Manchester law firms and thought the career would be interesting and offer lots of different opportunities. I was also very keen to travel and thought a commercial firm would offer the best chance to work abroad. All of those assumptions were correct!

I thought about lots of career options until choosing my A-Levels but after that was very focused on law. I did also consider becoming a barrister but decided that being a solicitor would offer more flexible career options over the long term.

It is always exciting to be working on cases that are front page news, and I have worked on a few of them. Although I have realised over the years that reporting is often inaccurate when you know the ins and outs of the cases! But some of the most interesting cases are the ones that are not in the public domain - that can be when lawyers are adding the most value - adeptly managing the risks for clients including the challenge of publicity.

I believe we should always challenge ourselves and continue to learn. I have been incredibly fortunate in my career in having been part of some of the most interesting issues in the financial services sector leading up to and then following the 2008 financial crisis. At the heart of a lot of those issues were cultural challenges faced by organisations. I decided in 2019 that my future interests lie in helping organisations to anticipate, interrogate and understand those risks, whilst also investigating issues with a clear focus on culture, diversity and inclusion.

We provide a unique service so competition is not really an issue and we are working with a wide range of law firms and clients. There are some parallels with what law firms offer but we are an alternative business structure authorised to provide legal services. That means we can bridge the gap between legal and consultancy advisory services and have a broader skill set beyond lawyers as part of our team. My business partner and I have always worked on a range of diversity issues as well as our day jobs (as litigation and employment lawyers), and we both held roles in-house and in private practice. We can therefore offer clients a different lens on the provision of advice."

## Working at O2, Arsenal and Uber

This next section shares the insight of Matthew Wilson, Associate General Counsel, EMEA & APAC at Uber. After leaving Baker McKenzie in 2008, Matthew moved out of private practice and shares his experience working in-house for over fifteen-years:

**About Matthew:**

"I would love to tell you that I wanted to be a lawyer from a young age and it was always something I planned on doing after university but that just is not the case. I was always interested in law and did work experience when I was at school in Oxfordshire at a local firm. But I was also interested in a host of other things when I was at university and I could have gone in a number of different directions whether that be banking, management consultancy, aviation or government and civil service roles.

It came to my third year at Durham University whilst I was studying Economics and Politics that I decided law was for me. During my final year you had the milk round of companies from the legal sector as well as other industries that would host events, typically in the evening. They would deliver their pitch, provide free food and drink, which is always a good thing when you are a student and are running out of cash, and more than anything I just really liked a lot of the people I met from the law firms.

I found the idea of continuing or extending my education whilst also learning a profession through the GDL was one that really appealed to me because it allowed me to continue travelling and learning with that guarantee that if you secured a training contract there would be a job at the end. The fact that with law and a lot of big firms you would get both the funding for the GDL and also that prospect of working on international work was really attractive. I went for it and I am very pleased that I did.

The biggest challenge for me was imposter syndrome: when you look around you and all the other people who are going for the same job as you are seemingly more qualified, have more natural aptitude and appear more intelligent. I thought 'how can I compete with those people?' Especially when I looked around as a non-lawyer - back then it was probably around 70% law students applying for training contracts and 30% non-law whereas now it is probably more 50/50.

I looked around and all these people knew partners at law firms and had law degrees and would drop names of family friends who were QC's and I felt that, in comparison, I had the imposter syndrome of not thinking I could compete because they seemed so certain and well connected to the industry that I were trying to get into. The thought is 'that is what I am competing with for a training contract.'

That said, somebody has to get these vacation schemes and training contracts, it might as well be you! You have to have humility of course, but you also need to be confident and believe in yourself. If I am being honest, I never had that same tunnel vision that a lot of the people around me seemed to have but what I always had was a real curiosity, not just about the law but about how the world works. For me, that is a big part of what law is really about. How human beings have decided to organise themselves – socially, economically, politically.

When I look back now, at the heart of most legal issues are people, and the choices those people make. So, having that natural curiosity does take you a very long way.

The legal industry can also be a bit of a black box when it comes to information.

Despite there being multiple sources of information about the legal sector and how many trainee solicitors' firms take on, what offices they have and how much you will earn, when I was applying to firms there really was not anywhere that gave you an honest, warts and all perspectives of what it is you are letting yourself in for when you sign up to be a lawyer. That is why this project is so interesting because looking back - hand on heart - when I was applying for training contracts and vacation schemes did I understand what being a lawyer actually was…no I did not. It sounded nice because it was seemingly well-paid and you had the potential to work on interesting matters and cases. I had a rough idea of what litigation and M&A work entailed. However, the nuts and bolts of what really goes into it does not become clear until you get to a law firm.

**The training contract:**

Back then there were some firms that did six seats rotating every four months and others that did four seats in six months. At Baker McKenzie, it was a firm that did four seats in six months. I started off in Dispute Resolution and then went to Private Equity and next moved onto Technology, Media and Telecoms and lastly Tax. All pretty broad.

I think the primary thing is that the seats that you do affect where you qualify into. Like anything else in life, they are just choices. What I would say about the seats you do, and that you put your hand up for, is that they are absolutely not one-way doors for your career. Do not let anyone tell you differently. Are they important? Yes, of course they are. Your time as a trainee solicitor sets the baseline for the rigour, technical and analytical skills - and emotional intelligence – that will come in handy for the rest of your career, whether that is law or not. That said, they are just a short moment in time where you get experience in different areas. They do not have to be a restriction to what you do next. Say you undertake the four seats that I did and then you want to become a competition lawyer – if you want to that badly enough, or decided to not be a lawyer at all and do something different, then you absolutely still can. Your training contract will still be helpful.

I knew that because I had very broad interests that a mix of broad practice areas to complete seats in would interest me and help keep my options as open as possible. That could be seen as not knowing what I wanted to do: you would be right and in some ways I still do not! Which is why I probably wanted to become a General Counsel because I am interested in a bit of everything rather than just interested in privacy or just interested in financial services! What I would say is you need a mix in the legal ecosystem - generalists and specialists - so, there is no right or wrong answer and nothing is set in stone because of your training contract choices. At the time when you are making your seat choices it may feel like they are one-way doors because they can feel competitive and like really massive decisions but you are not really closing anything off.

When you go through your career it is the skills you have developed and not necessarily the firm you trained at that determines the direction you go in and how successful you are. That is not just your legal skills but also the way in which you build and manage relationships and people. That is just as important as the legal skills and knowledge you develop. In the legal team here at Uber we have people that have come from magic circle firms as well as regional firms in Leeds and Newcastle. The team I look after here at Uber is seventy people across fifty countries and we have people from all over the world. People who trained and qualified in places like India, Jordan, Kenya, Poland, Spain, Japan as well as people qualified in a variety of jurisdictions who have moved to work at our offices in Amsterdam or the United States. So, my point is this: regardless of the path you take and the choices you make early in your career there is a great ability to still do whatever you want to do if you want to do it enough.

**Routes in-house:**

Thinking about moving from a private practice law firm to moving in-house, there are a variety of ways of doing it:

i. In-house training contracts - there are not many companies that offer trainee solicitors in-house but there still are some. We have a lawyer in our team at Uber who completed his training contract at Nike and I am aware of other companies that do offer training contracts. However, this is a niche option as companies rarely offer this and is still the exception.

ii. Apply for a qualified job. Qualifying at a law firm after your training contract and then applying for a job in-house. Typically, the most well-trodden route.

iii. Going on secondment, and then getting tapped up! Quite often trainee solicitors and young lawyers are poached from law firms' after or during secondments to client companies. This is one of the best ways to move in-house because during a secondment you build up that crucial relationship with an in-house team and it becomes an extended interview process where you can both size each other up. The client can decide whether you would be a great hire and you can have a good look at whether it is a place you would like to work and build a career.

iv. More and more you also have legal agencies like Axiom - this is where you are a qualified lawyer but for whatever reason you decide you do not want to tie yourself down working at a law firm or at an in-house position at one single company. So, what Axiom does is that you register with them and meet a certain quality requirement and then for want of a better word they 'pimp you out' to different companies on a periodic basis. This could be every three or six months to cover work by employees at their companies who are on annual or parental leave and there is a gap to be filled.

As much as I like variety, up to this point in my career, that last option is not one I have tried. I would not rule it out in the future but up to now, what has given me purpose has been different. I am very curious and all the businesses I have worked for have had a good level of variety.

However, I realised pretty early in my career that I am very mission driven. I like to feel as though I am part of something with a clear purpose that I buy into and have a sense of ownership and belonging - whether that is playing football for a team or whether it is being part of a company or organisation. That feeling of belonging and contributing to building something I am passionate about is what I really enjoy and what really gives me purpose.

Whenever I have been happiest in my life, I have had a good combination of pleasure and purpose in both my professional and personal lives. That is why I have not yet gone down the lawyers on demand route. That said, at a different point in my life I could see going down the route of doing a variety of different types of work at different companies would be fun but at this stage that feeling of having a mission and building something over a sustained period of time is what drives me. I have lots of friends that have done interim work though, and they have loved it and the freedom it gives you. Whatever you do, always think about your personality, what makes you happy and what gives you purpose.

After fifteen years of working in-house I can safely say it has changed massively since I started. Working in-house has become a separate and distinct career path now with very separate skill sets to the ones that you need in private practice. I have absolutely loved it but it will not be for everybody and you might perfect being a barrister or a solicitor in a private practice law firm. So, I would say think very carefully about how you want to work, what interests you and where and how you want to spend your working life. Then you should think about whether: (i) that is even as a lawyer and (ii) if so, what kind of law do you want to do every day. Is that legal research or do you enjoy working alongside a business more closely or do you enjoy standing on your feet arguing? All of these questions are really important for you to reflect on, to ensure you go in the direction you want to go in career wise.

**Skills required to become a great Trainee Solicitor:**

Emotional intelligence - if you can cultivate strong emotional intelligence and use it this will be the biggest skill you can have as a trainee solicitor (accepting that you would not be there if you did not have the baseline academic credentials). You need to recognise that by and large being a trainee solicitor is not (or at least should not be treated as) a zero-sum game. You have some trainee solicitors that come in and it is a competition from day one. I remember coming into my intake and feeling and seeing this competition between trainee solicitors. It is understandable as you know there are only a certain number of jobs at the end of the two years and only a certain number of roles in specific departments. I think it is important to remember that life does not start and end at the firm you train at and that the relationships you make during your training contract - including with your peers - are extremely important too.

It really is not a zero-sum game. You should of course go for what you want to do but I always think it is important not to trample on people on the way. You also need to be a bit like Jim Carrey in the film 'Yes Man'. By saying 'yes' to things you do not necessarily know where that is going to take you. It is where you get out of your comfort zone and learn though. Now, that does not just mean saying 'yes' to the good work that might come your way it is also about saying 'yes' to whatever people need you to do and taking pride in whatever that may be. If you have high standards on paginating a bundle or proof-reading a Sale and Purchase Agreement (M&A) it shows to supervisors that you are likely to have high standards on more complex work too.

Be curious, ask lots of questions and be helpful and demonstrate an ability to go further than just the question you have been asked. At Uber we call it peering round corners. If you see that there is a potential issue, then keep asking questions until you get to the bottom of it. I always tell people in our team when they arrive that there is no such thing as a stupid question - if you do not know something it is our responsibility, as a team, to make sure you have that knowledge so that you can advise properly and have everything you need to do your job. 'Why?' is the most important question in many cases because it allows you to get to the right answer and give the best advice - if you understand 'why' something is the way it is then it allows you to advise better. If you only understand the 'what' then your advice is not going to be as good.

Asking questions goes hand in hand with being honest about what you do not know. Probably still my worst experience as a lawyer was when I was a newly qualified solicitor and had a piece of privacy advice to do the first drafts which involved looking at the underlying privacy laws in the UK and how they apply to international companies. For one reason or another because of the way my training contract had gone I had never touched any privacy work before. I did not know where to start and I should have just asked more questions at the time and it was a really good learning experience because it is an area of the law where 'the why' really matters as well as the what. It made me miserable at the time and I could have handled it better.

**Benefits of training in-house:**

The immediate thing that comes to mind is the tension of legal rigour versus commerciality. For me, commerciality will come with experience anyway. Whether that is experience in private practice or in-house you are going to develop that commercial experience over time with the increasing number of situations you see. It is much easier (and in my view better) to develop the rigour earlier in your career. Rigour includes attention to detail, the ability to go deep on a legal question or problem by pulling at the threads and being in private practice, with that law firm environment, really helps you do that and develop those skills. This is because when you are in that an in-house environment you might have thirty to forty different things on your to-do list all with different clients who are demanding your time. That rigour is much harder to develop and make second nature later in your career. In my current role I can go deep on issues if needed but may choose not to because the likely financial, operational or legal risks do not demand it.

**Skills required in-house:**

I think the biggest one we have already touched on - emotional intelligence. As a trainee solicitor I figured out fairly on that having an ability to get on with others and be interested in a number of areas goes a long way towards both enjoying and effectively doing your job. Finding ways to work with everyone is so important - whether you 'like' them or not: that does not mean being a pushover but it does mean you have to treat people and deal with people differently, recognising people's motivations and priorities will also allow you to succeed and do your job to the best of your ability.

**Moving from Baker McKenzie to O2:**

At that time there was not a problem finding a job, there were lots out there. The biggest problem or issue was twofold: first, how do you pick the right role and, second, what is this role going to actually mean for me in the future? Those two things are a bit intertwined of course. All I tried to do was look for an industry that I thought as going to be relevant for the next five to ten years, was growing quickly and was going to be interesting.

O2 was perfect for that because the iPhone had just arrived, Android was starting up, as was the digital delivery of content, all of which sped up technological change at a rapid rate. Back then it was still 2G technology (or GPRS) then it went 3G, 4G and we are now into 5G. How we use the airwaves and radio spectrum was a big debate that I managed to get involved in and learnt from some super smart people, alongside having a front row seat on how social media and mobile devices were affecting our daily lives and interactions with each other. I found that hugely interesting so it was a great place to work.

Also, the fact that O2 were based West of London at the time was a great location for my wife and I and the team was big enough that it had a little bit of that private practice flavour to it as well as we had had specialists in areas like privacy, regulatory, litigation, IP and employment to learn from and get advice on as well as there being a broad variety of work.

The biggest challenge generally about going in-house was that suddenly you had this independence and freedom that you did not have in private practice. In private practice your work as a trainee solicitor tends to get checked before it goes out. As a lawyer working in house it is very different. When a client comes to you, they do not see you as a one or two-year qualified lawyer - instead they just see you as a lawyer who has the legal training to answer any question they may have. That can be liberating, which it was, but it can also be daunting especially when there is a big impact associated with a case or deal you are working.

At O2, I went in and I was a lawyer in the Commercial Team. The great thing about being that was that I had the chance to get involved with a whole range of areas of the business and lots of different types of legal issues, included:

i. Technology infrastructure projects like radio spectrum and broadband.
ii. Content deals with music labels where we were selling ringtones and music through your phone.
iii. Partnership deals with the likes of Google for things like search functionality to be preinstalled on your phone.
iv. Preinstallation of games.
v. Marketing campaigns – i.e. at O2 I had to do the work behind the scenes for things like prize giveaways and competitions.
vi. Sponsorship deals – i.e. We had one with Arsenal and England Rugby, did things with the O2 Arena.

vii.     Day to day regulatory issues with Ofcom, litigation and privacy issues with the ICO.

At two or three years qualified that exposure was great. At the time, O2 acquired a company called Be Broadband and I was the lawyer who was in charge of looking after that part of the business. Then a couple of years into O2 my brilliant boss Alison moved to Ireland for a year and then went on maternity leave so the team (led by Ed Smith and Kate Jarvis at the time) asked me to step up to do her job. It was very daunting and stretching at the time but it was an amazing experience.

As a result, I moved up to a more senior position and was given greater opportunities to work across different areas of the company. For instance, O2 bought Jajah which was a company based in Silicon Valley for $300 million. That was my first experience of Silicon Valley and I was part of the integration team that was part of bringing Jajah into the Telefonica group. So absolutely brilliant experience at that point in my career. I also did a lot of work in China and South America after returning to O2 having left to go to Arsenal for a few years.

**Moving from O2 to Arsenal:**

The job was a ton of fun. I have been a fan since I was a young kid and it was one of those opportunities that I could not turn down. It was a great place full of excellent people. The work ranged from helping out on things like player transfers and stadium events to sponsorship contracts and IP enforcement. I remember a deal for a series of Coldplay concerts I was involved with at the Emirates which was good fun. I was also involved with ticketing terms and conditions as well as licencing the Arsenal brand to go on merchandise to then be sold across the world. I also would deal with arrangements to do with the Arsenal website, online store and many other areas.

I adored the job but found that I probably was not learning at the same pace that I had been when I was at O2. I decided to leave Arsenal to go back to O2 because it was the right thing for me to do at the time in my career despite the fact that I loved it there. I would not have been able to do the job I do now at Uber had I not left Arsenal to go back to O2. That was a big and difficult choice for me and took my career in a different direction.

**Working at Uber:**

If I am very honest, Uber has been the job of a lifetime. I remember using Uber back in 2013 in San Francisco fairly soon after it first started. I was over there with Telefonica. I met up with a friend and he said let's get an Uber to the restaurant we were going to. He got his phone out, the car arrived and we got to the restaurant and I remember thinking at the time this is pretty magical - tap a button, get a ride. So, when a role came up in 2015 in the UK for Uber's first legal director in the UK it was too good of an opportunity to turn down. It was a big career risk at the time because I was going to be making less money and I had a team of fifteen at that time whereas at Uber I was going to be solo in a fast-paced environment in an office above a Tesco Metro round the back of Kings Cross Station!

At the time the company was really well funded by really serious Silicon Valley investors but had an aggressive risk appetite and there was no guarantee that it was going to continue to be a success and grow. That said, I was really excited by the mission and I always remember going for my interview with the General Manager of Uber UK and I always remember after the interview walking down the staircase and coming up there was this guy and he had his TFL private hire papers in one hand to sign up for Uber and what must have been his young daughter in the other. I just remember thinking if this company could be available all over the world and it makes it easier for people to make money for themselves and their families then that cannot be a bad thing and if I could play some kind of role in making sure those people can make a decent living in a flexible way while enabling people to move around cities more easily that must actually be a very good thing. I was inspired by that mission and still am today.

The whole business model is based on supply and demand and therefore is hugely interesting (for someone with an Economics and Politics degree!). What do I actually do? The team handles everything that comes in the door - my role when I started was to grow the team and I hired four really brilliant lawyers early on who are all still at Uber today. As time went on I was given more countries and people to look after.

We hit 2017 and my boss at the time left and they asked me to look after the EMEA team (Europe, Middle East and Africa). We grew that from around twenty-five people to approximately sixty people and then I was asked to look after APAC about a year ago. So, it has been incredible and I do know I have been very lucky. In terms of what my responsibilities are now day to day, my first priority is to try and make sure the environment we have for the team allows them to work cohesively, communicate effectively and do their best work so we have a happy, healthy team who do a great job for Uber.

In terms of the business side of things we look after the provision of all legal advice for the business. Whether that is how the Uber App works, reviewing marketing, litigation and ensuring we have the license and right to operate in different countries we work in, or doing deals with restaurants for UberEATS - we get involved in all of it, as well as advising on the relationships we have with drivers and couriers.

One of things I am most proud of at Uber so far was when we helped out in the efforts to take the company public on the New York stock exchange in 2019. That was incredible.

The business model is broadly the same for rides and Eats on Uber - the drivers will charge the rider say £10 and we will take a 25% cut for linking these people with the customers. On Eats, there are small differences as there are restaurants, couriers and eaters! The technology all works in a way that tries to be as efficient as possible and reduce the amount of time that a driver does not have a person in a car or that courier does not have a delivery to make. This maximises the amount of time the courier or driver is making money for themselves. So, the business is fascinating but there have of course been some well-documented challenges along the way! We went through a real crisis in 2017 so my role was very much to help manage that situation along with the rest of our team and the rest of the leadership team.

**In-house highlight:**

The experience at Uber from being a scrappy start transitioning to become a public listed company and dealing with that pressure of high growth and crisis management in the public eye was by far the most interesting experience. Being part of the leadership team that deals with events such as COVID-19 and attempted terrorist attacks has been fascinating and rewarding.

At Arsenal I had two highlights. One was organising those Coldplay concerts which was pretty cool. The second thing was just getting to know the inner workings of a football club and meeting the people that dedicate their lives to go above and beyond for a sport and club they are so passionate about was amazing. I could have very easily and happily stayed at Arsenal for the rest of my career. For one reason or another it just did not work out that way.

The biggest highlight I have had in my career actually is not a legal one at all. It is the fact that through my jobs whether it has been at Baker McKenzie, O2, Arsenal or Uber I have had the privilege of being able to travel the world. That is just amazing because if you had said to me when I was ten years old growing up in north west London that as part of my job I would travel to India, Nigeria and South Africa, China, Hong Kong, all around Europe, Argentina and Brazil I would not have believed you. It is not just that I was able to travel to those places it was that I was able to meet people there, learn and experience their cultures, share experiences and get a better insight into how the world works. I really realised that over the last six months because of COVID-19 and feel very lucky to have been able to do so much travel for my job. Like I said, it is a privilege.

**What to think about when making a move:**

It really comes down to your own individual personality. Some people enjoy the academic side of being in private practice whereas some people enjoy the steady diet of big deals and being associated with complicated deals that you get at the big law firms. In-house you get to work on big deals but it is different because you are focused on the mission of the company. For instance, for Uber I worked to buy a Middle Eastern company called Careem, which was valued over $3bn, I worked on the Yandex deal which was worth over $3bn as well, and we had one of the biggest ever IPO's in history.

However, those big deals are the exceptions in-house - day to day you are working on all kinds of things across the business to ensure it runs effectively. For some people that does not suit their personality because they just like to work on headline-grabbing deals or have one or two cases to focus on at a time. Most in-house lawyers will be working on thirty or forty different things at any time, which can be anything from individual personal injury claims in Romania, regulatory change in Lagos, commercial deals in the Netherlands all the way through to big pieces of M&A and I just love that variety.

When you go into most house jobs it is a variety that you are going to get and you need to be willing to roll your sleeves up and do the work needed and not just the things you want to do. The advantages are that you get all that visibility and variety of working in-house and you also tend to have more control over your work-life balance as a result - including over where and when you work. You are typically very close to the business by working in-house and 'normal' people - not just surrounded by lawyers! The potential disadvantages are that the buck stops with you - if the business wants some legal advice on any issue they expect you to be able to provide it whether it is an area of law that you enjoy or not. Depending on the type of organisation you are in, the business might not have the ability or financial resources to outsource legal advice to private practice firms and therefore you will be expected to make a judgement call on behalf of the business. That is also a difference because you have a bit more time in private practice to reflect and think about questions that are asked whereas you have to make a huge number of decisions very quickly every single day when you are in an in-house environment. You need to be pretty resilient and have good judgment.

**Non-law related highlights:**

I managed a football team for years when I was in my early thirties. Why is that the most interesting for me? What was great about that was that at a relatively young age it allowed me to test out and experiment with my leadership style. It allowed me to have that pressure to deliver every week when you have to get fourteen or fifteen guys together every Saturday and get them to work as a cohesive team or unit and build team spirit. Before I had any sizable team to manage at work it was a really great way of testing out management and leadership strategies from a people point of view, learning how you motivate people and how you get them to work with each other. This has enabled me to translate over a lot of skills to my job and how I manage my teams now.

I am secretly incredibly competitive and hate losing so whereas generally I am a kind and empathetic leader but there is also a competitive element and undercurrent where I want to succeed and win as a team. How that manifests itself and how you inspire your teams can vary wildly. One of the reasons why Arsene Wenger was such a successful leader was because he was very careful about when he would scream and shout and throw tea cups. He would not do it very often at all and may only do it once a season but when he did it would have a real impact. I do not scream and shout or throw tea cups (HR are generally glad about that) but when I do get tougher than people know that it is serious because my normal way of operating is calm, tolerant and friendly. As a leader you always want to remain authentic to your teams and be approachable and create the right kind of environment where you are leading by consent and not fear. That has always been very important to me.

**Role model:**

For me my role model is my dad and there are a few different reasons for that. The first is that he has always prioritised his family and put me, my mum and my brother (and now his grandchildren!) first. He is retired now but when he was a teacher and then headmaster - he always had a strong work ethic. I remember when I was little in London and him getting up early in the morning, jumping on the Central Line to teach at a school near Tower Bridge and then getting home relatively late at night every day for years.

My dad taught me about being resilient. He went from being a teacher to a deputy head to being a headmaster but did not get that headmaster role first time and taught me that you need to keep trying and persevering and that even if you do not succeed it is okay, but if you believe in something enough and want it enough to persevere because it will happen. He taught me about humility but also the importance of getting along with people from all different cultures, personalities and walks of life.

You need to be really careful about how you treat people on the way up because you never know when you come across them again. No matter how well you think your life or career is going it might not be one day. Every interaction you have with every person matters. That is something that my dad always did brilliantly – whether you were an MP or a governor or a member of his leadership team or if you were the receptionist, caretaker or worked in the kitchens he treated everyone with equal value and importance. And that is something I have always tried to do too."

# Chapter 6: Understanding Diversity & Inclusion in the Legal Sector

This chapter showcases a variety of insight from diverse backgrounds in an effort to connect you with the profession you either are aspiring to enter or are currently in. As a disclaimer, this chapter is by no means a one-stop-shop for every barrier an individual faced entering the profession. This would be impossible as everyone has a different journey. Instead, I aim to share the insight of resilient individuals who have succeeded in the legal profession and overcome circumstances that go against the grain.

**What does diversity mean:**

Simon Colvin explains that "diversity means having anyone who turns up to work be themselves and be treated in exactly the same way no matter who they are, what they look like or what their background is, and that it makes no difference as to how they can progress through their careers. Diversity is pure equal treatment and acceptance of everyone for what they are and who they are no matter how physically able they are or what sexual orientation or ethnicity they are. None of that should matter when you come into the workforce because at the end of the day we sit here and we use what is and the grey matter and everyone should be given equal treatment for that."

**What does diversity mean in practice:**

To get the ball rolling I turn to Vaibhav Adlakha who is an Associate at Reed Smith. Vaibhav has cerebral palsy and is a quadriplegic. Meaning that he has limited movement in his arms and legs and required to use a wheelchair. However, Vaibhav's proudest achievement is that he has become known "more for my legal work than for the fact that I have a disability and use a wheelchair." Over to Vaibhav for his experience entering the profession:

"If I could summarise my journey in a few words, it has been a difficult path as well as an enlightening one. During this process, I have learnt more about myself and understood the type of lawyer I want to be. I also realized that it is important to find a firm that matches your ambitions with the requirement of the business, so that both can collaborate. I had to figure out how I would fit within the legal environment. It has been tough, because at the time I was looking for training contracts, I did not consider all the aspects of being a lawyer and the environment I want to be in. Hence, it took quite a long time for me to understand how law firms differ from one another and how not all firms fit everyone.

When I was first applying to law firms, I did not understand aspects of what commercial law firms do and what that entails. The work experience I gained before going into the profession made me appreciate and understand commercial law. During this time, I actually comprehended that it is all about building the brand of the client helping them to achieve their goals and objectives throughout the life cycle of the business.

Thus, as the business grows so do you and your brand become synonymous with theirs. In this respect, I have enjoyed building relationships and working in partnership with clients. When I first started the profession, I just wanted a firm to give me an opportunity to have a career. However, having had a break from applying and then trying again, I started to look for a firm that matched what I wanted to achieve from the profession. I was also looking for a firm that focused on their people as much as they do on their clients. In other words, as the firm grows and develops the brand of the firm becomes synonymous with the brand of the people at that firm. I think it is time that firms adapt themselves to accommodate the talent that they want in the same way they would for their clients.

I wanted to be a lawyer since I was seventeen. This came from my experience, participating in the Model United Nations conferences. I worked as an advocate, Judge and the presiding judge at these conferences and found the whole experience very interesting, challenging and dynamic. However, when I was unsuccessful in obtaining a training contract, I did consider other professions where I could use my legal skills. I worked with the Dutch government (Environment Ministry and Competition Authority) and other organisations (Human Rights) in the Netherlands. I also considered Human Resources and a career as a legal analyst. All of these considerations had a direct relationship with law because I knew it was where I wanted to pursue a career. Having stepped out of the legal profession, I missed the commercial legal sector and that is why I came back.

In terms of my career being an advisory lawyer is quite interesting because, compared to other aspects of the law, you are a bridge between knowing what the client's ambitions are and how they can be achieved within the sphere of the law. For instance, if a client wants to buy a stake in another company, it is good for them to create synergies but they have to be able to do so within the framework of the competition law paradigm.

My responsibilities have an international element to them. I look at transactions in terms of monopolisation, cartels, abuse of dominance, national security, state aid and dawn raids. We look at all the possible anti-competitive issues, which could arise from the objectives of the client.

I also deal with marketing of funds in different jurisdictions for financial regulation, which involves understanding the type of funds companies wish to market as well as the type of investor. Just like in competition law, you have to understand the industry in which they operate.

There is a lot of practical and creative analysis involved to help clients achieve their objectives within the framework of the law. A career highlight for me has been the ability to establish client relationships myself - the feeling is second to none. The biggest sense of achievement is when the client directly calls you to find a solution. This has happened both as a trainee solicitor and as an associate. Having the ability to solve complex issues and answer bespoke questions, where the issue has never been dealt with before or there is no precedent for it, has been the most exhilarating part of being a lawyer for me. Another biggest achievement also has been to become known more for my legal work than for the fact that I have a disability and use a wheelchair.

My training contract at Reed Smith has been a very interesting experience. In the beginning, I did not have any idea what type of lawyer I wanted to be. Having the opportunity to explore four varying seats: shipping admiralty, banking, competition and financial regulation, was quite helpful to figure out not only the type of lawyer I wanted to be but also my strengths/skills and where they matched best. I was fortunate to work and train with people who are experts in their field, and I was able to learn and gain valuable skills under their guidance.

What I enjoy about Competition and Financial Regulation is the fact that they have an international element to them. No two questions are ever the same and they can apply to any industry, so you have to be able to think more creatively than in many other practice areas. My work consists of areas such as national security, public procurement, state aid, fund marketing for financial regulations and merger control. Not all these areas are straightforward, especially in advisory, because you have to understand the industry before you can apply the law.

Some of the skills I have learnt, thus far during my time at Reed Smith, are attention to detail, legal drafting and being able to provide practical solutions to client issues. I also learnt to understand that lawyers are in a service industry so the main goal should be to fulfil client ambitions as well as to be honest about when things are possible and when they are not. I learnt to think in a practical way and to try to find solutions on my own. I was encouraged by supervisors to analyse complex issues, to communicate my thoughts and help guide clients to the best solutions. This is the best kind of training to ensure one develops a commercial mind-set and attention to detail but at the same time learn to think more independently.

The best environment to work in depends on what type of lawyer you want to be and what your personal preferences may be. My first seat was in a small specialist team, the second seat was in a bigger team, and my third and fourth were again with small specialist teams. For me, being in a smaller team worked well for my training because I was integrated into the team right from the beginning and given extensive responsibility. By the time I finished my training contract, I was already taking the lead on certain issues and contributing equally with other members of the team.

The responsibilities as a newly qualified solicitor do change to some extent but not drastically, if you qualify in the same smaller team where you trained. There is more trust in you to be able to provide advice independently and to lead transactions. One of the key things that my partner said to me when I first started as an associate was that 'we are one team'. Furthermore, you are trying to build your own personal identity as an associate but that confidence level comes in time and with experience. However, because I was in smaller teams for my final two seats, I was already getting some of the responsibilities that an associate would get and therefore the transition was not as big for me.

My advice to final seat trainee solicitors is to enjoy the experience and learning without worrying about getting a job at your firm. Understand what type of lawyer you want to be and where you want to spend your career. By now, you should already know what area of law you want to specialize in and what kind of work you want to do for the rest of your career. Focus on trying to perfect the skills that you have learnt throughout your training contract and prepare yourself for the future environment. Once you know what kind of lawyer you want to be, nothing can stop you from finding the right kind of environment you want to be in."

## How to enter the profession with a disability:

This is a question that aspiring solicitors consider when they are attempting to secure a training contract. However, for those struggling with a particular barrier, Vaibhav shares his experience entering the profession in this section and reflects on what he wished to have been told:

"If I could go back and give myself a piece of advice, I would say enjoy the journey of learning and acquiring skills more than the desire to get to the final destination. Enjoy every experience you can get because, more often than not, we focus on becoming a lawyer or getting a training contract and forget about gaining skills. It was only after many rejections and not getting a training contract did I understand, it was those learning experiences that actually prepared me better for the profession I wanted to pursue. Hence, enjoy every experience, because no experience is a bad one as it teaches a special skill, whether working at an NGO or as a retailer.

It is more important to enjoy the journey of self-exploration rather than simply focusing on the final destination because that is sometimes more exciting than the final destination. Do not be afraid to fail because as Samuel Beckett says 'Try Again. Fail Again. Fail Better.' Every time you fail, try to fail better than the last because that is the only way you will achieve success.

When I was coming back into the legal profession, Reed Smith was my last shot. At the time when I was applying to Reed Smith for a training contract, I did not know that they would be the perfect firm for me. However, when I got to the interview, I got the impression that they were focusing on what I could do rather than what I could not. The premise at which they started the interview was looking at my ability and whether I was good for the job rather than my disability and why I would not be able to do it. The other major factor throughout my time at Reed Smith was the mental aspect and adjustments of the firm for my disability. They were willing to adapt themselves to create a position in a way that allowed me to flourish and contribute.

I have cerebral palsy and am quadriplegic. This means that I have limited movement in my arms and legs and am required to use a wheelchair. All adaptations were made to suit my needs. The firm insisted by giving me a personal assistant to help me with any physical issues which enabled me to operate at the same level as other trainee solicitors and associates. The majority of law firms are willing to make a physical adjustment to help people with a disability, but Reed Smith focused on my capability and strengths.

The one thing I would say is that the legal profession is a hard one for people with disabilities. The expectation is always that law firms have to change and to focus on the ability of an individual. While that is true and I want law firms to have a better understanding, it is equally important for people with a disability to understand what working in a law firm entails. Each individual with a disability needs different accommodations and so, it can be difficult for law firms to know how to adapt themselves to create the perfect environment.

Hence, it is important for people with disabilities to understand how their limitations would affect them in the workplace so that you can collaborate with the firm to find a perfect solution. Law firms must work towards understanding the disability of each individual in trying to create a level playing field for them. However, people with disability will also have a better experience if they try to understand the kind of environment they are going into. They must also understand what might work best for both the business needs of the company and the aspirations of the individual.

The advice I would give is to know what your ability is rather than what your disability. Know how you are going to work within the profession and how your disability will affect the environment, you want to be in. For example, in the beginning I thought I could be a good transactional lawyer but soon found out that the pace of transactional work was not for me. Therefore, one needs to understand what expectations the clients may have and how can you fulfil those expectations. At the end of the day, you want to be treated the same as everyone else and have the same expectations from clients and colleagues. Which is why it is important to know how your disability works and how you are able to do the work that is expected of you with the limitations that you have, this is the key to entering the profession. The journey from disability to ability is a tough one so be sure to have a good support network around you as they will advise you further on what the best environment might be for you.

My role model is every person who went the extra mile and who went against the grain of others around them in society to give people like me a shot. If it were not for teachers in my school who said, 'I want him in my class and we will give him the extra time to ensure he can do the best he can', I would not have thought I could be a lawyer. If it were not for teachers and my parents putting the extra time and effort in to ensure I do my best, I would not be at a law firm. If it were not for my colleagues being willing to adjust to my disability, I would not have succeeded in the way that I have. My role models are all of those who have supported me from when I started to where I am now, those who have been able to think outside the box and think of doing things differently than how they have traditionally been done and all those who gave me a chance."

## Disability in the legal sector from Carolyn Pepper, Partner at Reed Smith and co-chair of the disability inclusion group LEADRS:

"Diversity in the workplace means bringing breadth of experience and breadth of thought to the workplace. I think in many cases there has always been an underlying wish to do the right thing in terms of hiring and career advancement but what has changed over the years is the harnessing of those intentions in the form of structured and organised inclusion groups which drive forward the firm's intentions.

My own view is that spending too much time discussing or thinking about the obstacles to creating a diverse workforce may not be the most productive use of time. The legal industry needs to act. We should focus on the opportunities and not the challenges.

Making conscious hiring decisions is key. If there is limited diversity among the people being hired, we need to ask tough questions about why that is and then do something to remove the barriers. We need to promote (in both senses of the word) diverse talent.

I was the first lawyer in my family (one of my four sisters is also a lawyer) and I do not come from a wealthy background. I was fortunate, however, to come from a family that values education, diversity, a strong work ethic and, given that the female to male ratio in my household was 6:1, a family that never doubted that women can achieve anything that they want to.

When I first arrived in the City, I knew nothing at all about the City. I was worried that I would be the only non-Oxbridge graduate and that I might not be as good as the other trainee solicitors. I decided that I would just enjoy the experience, rely on my natural optimism, work hard and see what happened.

I think work experience is key and that we need to give people from different backgrounds the opportunity to see what working in a larger law firm is actually like so that they know that there are opportunities for people from all backgrounds and that they can succeed and thrive.

Reed Smith has the Disability Business Inclusion Group, LEADRS and the firm believes that disability diversity is a key component of any diversity and inclusion strategy. Generally speaking, progress on diversity in the legal and other industries is slow but recent improvements in technology and flexible home working make a big difference to people with disabilities. That said, inclusion of people with disabilities in workplaces generally still has some way to go.

Some businesses fear that employing people with disabilities will be costly. That has not been our experience. Once people realise the benefits that people with disabilities bring to the workplace, perceptions will begin to change."

## How to enter the legal profession as a member of the LGBT+ community:

The next topic for this chapter that I wanted to focus on was sharing the perspective of a lawyer from the LGBT+ community. With this being a topic discussed at many law firms, I thought it would be important to highlight the experience of a lawyer who entered the legal profession to shed perspective on the positive progress made in recent years, but also what needs to be changed to increase accessibility and inclusivity. I turn to Scott Halliday who is an academic writer and Associate Family Law Solicitor at Irwin Mitchell in London and Leeds:

"My clients are not limited to those cities as a lot of my work is referred to me directly by contacts and past clients passing on my details. My clients increasingly come from across the country and internationally.

I enjoy international work and meeting clients from different parts of the country often with different legal concerns and priorities. I work on a range of family law issues, with a particular emphasis on divorce/dissolution, the financial consequences of relationship breakdown and complex private law children disputes.

The financial work is often complicated. I regularly represent high-net-worth individuals and/or their spouse and deal with issues around high incomes, spousal maintenance, business interests, multiple properties, assets held abroad, valuable pensions and other assets such as art or jewellery. In respect of children, I undertake a wide range of legal work, but most notably international/internal relocation of children, abduction of children and/or cases with an intractable dispute which the Court has to determine. This is usually around very serious allegations of abuse.

Before practice I graduated with a First-Class Honours degree in Law LLB in 2013 at the University of York. Whilst at York, in 2012, I obtained a prestigious scholarship which enabled me to attend the international summer institute at Seoul National University (SNU) in South Korea. The summer institute at SNU involved lectures and extensive reading/essay writing for two months. I studied international comparative politics, human rights and philosophy. I also explored Seoul and wider South Korea - it was a very immersive and fast paced time. It was an exciting period.

I graduated from SNU with a much deeper understanding of philosophy and politics, which at least intellectually informed my understanding of law. The style of teaching was often Socratic, I was often debating issues with my contemporaries from leading universities like Harvard, Princeton and Oxbridge. On my return I was fortunate to then graduate and be appointed as a Bridge Fund Scholar of Law at the University of York in 2013-2014. I went on to obtain an LLM International Human Rights Law and Practice. My LLM was wide ranging, but I focused heavily on human rights defenders, the Rwandan Genocide, the responsibility to protect doctrine as well as LGBT+ human rights issues. My final thesis focused on the emergence, as it was then, of same-sex marriage as a European human rights issue.

It was around the time I sat my finals as an undergraduate that I was part of a Vacation Scheme at Irwin Mitchell in Sheffield. I was twenty years old at the time. It was a brilliant, if not stressful, experience. I think it is fair to say that anyone at that age in a large law firm would find the process stressful. It was such a big opportunity, in truth, at still a very young age. I was offered a training contract at the end of the vacation scheme. I lived in Leeds whilst studying the LPC; during this period, I also lectured in Law and Society at the University of York Law School and worked at an NGO on Pro Bono LGBT+ Asylum law.

**Working at Irwin Mitchell:**

I had always wanted to work in a large national firm. The networks and opportunities available in firms of this nature appealed to me. Irwin Mitchell is a full service large national law firm. The firm is well established in the market as a leader. It has great strength and depths. The longer I am at the firm the more I see it and the more I realise how much it adds to client experience/the quality of service provided. There are very few firms who offer at our standard the full range of legal services.

I knew that I wanted to work with individuals and resolve personal disputes about people and lives; I was never attracted to corporate work in that sense. That said a lot of my clients are business owners and/or senior figures in successful companies/the wider professions and so I often advise on these issues and the division of assets and income from this perspective. I like the fusion of personal services and business that financial family law work generates.

When I applied to Irwin Mitchell it was one of four training contracts that I applied for as an undergraduate. I applied and did not progress very far whilst a second year undergraduate. I applied to the same firms in my final year as an undergraduate and ultimately then secured a training contract. When I attended the assessment centre at Irwin Mitchell I immediately got a sense that the firm was packed with extremely talented people who were also crucially human. I had on occasion felt that I would not fit into a corporate environment and had earlier in my studies considered progressing with a research post/PhD. I enjoyed studying and research. I was also working class, the first generation to attend university in my family and a gay man. The legal profession at that time was still, it felt to me, not a space where I could genuinely thrive. In truth at that stage I was pessimistic as to whether or not I could secure a training contract.

In the end, after much deliberation, I decided I had to try and if I was going to try then I wanted to join a firm that offered me high-quality training and work. I also decided that I needed to be a lawyer for a period and experience the law in practice before I could research and comment on the profession/law in academia.

I was drawn to Irwin Mitchell's identity during the recruitment process, it felt like the firm was packed with really talented people who strived for success, but crucially who were also humorous and warm. I liked the combination. I wanted to be part of a diverse workforce as I was very aware of my own diversity. I cannot say that the environment at Irwin Mitchell is different or better than other firms; I have always worked at Irwin Mitchell. What I can say is that the firm will suit candidates who wish to be the very best at what they do, but who also have personality and want to be authentic.

I work in London and Leeds week to week. It is rather busy and hectic, but I enjoy the fast-paced nature of the work and spending time in both cities. One of the best aspects of Family Law work is the great variety of clients - in terms of legal issues they face; professional background; their motivations and life story. It is a real privilege to be a trusted adviser and guide client's often in high conflict litigation. I always thought that I would like to be a litigator as I enjoy thinking and strategy as well as constructing arguments/being analytical. It is a key skill for a family lawyer.

I trained for one year initially in Sheffield. I lived and worked in Sheffield during that period - it was a completely new city to me and I enjoyed my time there, especially in Family Law. I also worked in human rights law and medical law for short periods. I then moved to Leeds to complete my training in 2016 and qualified into Family Law in 2017.

Leeds is a great legal centre with lots of quality law firms and the city has a real identity. I was a solicitor for just over two years and then promoted to an associate solicitor in 2019. I was able to promote, I think on reflection, as I had successfully co-ordinated a string of complex cases that ran to trial and had very good outcomes. These cases included abduction work, relocation of children, same-sex family law issues and a few big money finance cases. In late 2018 I also started to generate much more of my own work with referrals. This culminated in late 2018 when I was shortlisted at the Yorkshire Legal Awards for Rising Star, for lawyers under the age of thirty-five, when I was just twenty-six. In late 2019 I moved to London and now I share my time week to week between London and Leeds.

I am increasingly doing a lot of LGBT+ family finance and children law work as I have particular expertise in this area so clients are often referred to me from cities like London, Manchester and Leeds. I am responsible for my own caseload day to day which is a mix of dealing with financial matters on separation and children law issues. I tend to do some international work within my case law, be it international finances on divorce/dissolution or international children law work like relocation of children or abduction.

**What are some of your career highlights:**

I have been asked to reflect on some career highlights to date. It is tough to know exactly what to say, but I have set out below some real highlights:

i. I had a series of international abduction cases in the High Court in London 2018-2019 which were very fast paced and tense, but on each occasion, we succeeded and the children remained in England. It was so satisfying given the stakes were so high and outcome so binary.

ii. There was also a proposed permanent international relocation of a child in the High Court to a non-Hague Convention state which ran to a contested week-long final hearing and our client succeeded to resist the move.

iii. A final hearing on financial matters upon divorce also comes to mind where the Judge, in a finely balanced high value case, agreed with our client's proposals and made a considerable costs order against the other side.

iv. Being appointed to the Law Society LGBT+ National Committee on Chancery Lane in 2019 was a real honour. It is such a privilege to work with the committee who are extremely bright, committed and able. We typically advocate for LGBT+ lawyers across the country through the Law Society; speak at expert events; raise awareness; support law firms and lawyers to create internal networks and sometimes training materials. I sit on several sub-committees, a focus of mine at present in transgender and non-binary issues in the law.

I have also advised/continue to advise on a landmark appeal case which deals with human rights and family law issues for LGBT+ people.

I would also say that a real highlight for me has been finding colleagues who share you goals and aspirations. It is so important that you try, as quickly as possible to surround yourself with link minded people. Do not misunderstand me, you will not find lots of people who think exactly in the same way about everything - It would be no fun at all if that was the case. But as you develop your practice you need support and guidance from people further on in their careers.

You should in my view make a real effort to identify those people quite early, if possible, in your career. They will inspire you to be your very best as you develop. It will really serve you well. You need colleagues and people in your wider professional network to encourage and support you as you develop. Think of it like a professional mentor or set of mentors. I still on occasion would pick up the phone to my very first supervisor in Family Law if I am puzzled by a case or want to discuss the pros and cons of possible next steps on a case. The support she gave me when I started still inspires me now.

In recent years the Law Society LGBT+ National Committee has also given me an opportunity to work with and become friends with genuine pioneering lawyers who inspire me. You cannot put a price on those types of connections and that sense of support. What I would also say is that the very best privilege, which I am starting to learn now more recently, is that once you are more senior and have developed your practice you then become the mentor figure. I am thrilled and enjoy working with colleagues on their development in family law. It is so satisfying to see colleagues succeed and to be part of their journey. But, also, more widely in terms of progressing wider interests like diversity in the profession or charity work. I also undertake a range of mentor roles now. I currently have three mentees who are really all very interesting and destined for great things.

**The importance of diversity and inclusion:**

It is essential for the legal profession to represent, as much as is possible, the people that it serves – the population. It is also essential that the legal profession is meritocratic and that opportunities and career growth are not limited. If you work really very hard consistently over a period of time and generate positive results for clients and your firm you deserve to be rewarded and be recognised.

It is a misnomer to suggest that there are insufficient numbers of people from diverse backgrounds who are well placed to excel in the legal profession. There are more than enough capable people from different diversity strands. It is a lack of opportunity not a lack of numbers which hold back progress and stifles meritocracy. It is the responsibility of the profession to make the case within schools and universities early on that the profession is open and actively wants to attract diverse talent. It is of course more complex that just that, but it is certainly a start. The profession must be understood and open to anyone who has the skills or strives to develop the skills to be involved.

I am interested in the full range of diversities and enthusiastic about widening participation. I am working class. I am the first generation in my family to attend university. I am a gay man. I only say this as these characteristics, especially when I was more junior, impacted on how I felt and how I saw myself in the law. The reality is that I was anxious about even attempting to enter the legal profession whilst I was an undergraduate. I did not want to disappoint myself or put myself in the public sphere to be rejected. It felt like it would take an enormous leap of faith to enter the profession twofold: (i) for me to have the nerve to apply and somehow succeed with an application; and (ii) for a law firm to recognise my academic talent and wider skills set and see that as of value.

I am disappointed to reflect on my experience in that way now, but it seems right to me to say it out loud in a book like this to try and educate and encourage others not to feel the same. If this sentiment does resonate then do not hesitate to move beyond it and pursue your ambitions. I should also note my reflections are now a decade old. There is already, excitedly, a new generation, younger than me, just starting to study at university/apply to enter the profession. To give one example Queer Lawyers of Tomorrow are a new group of students who want to address diversity for LGBT+ students. I work with them often on such issues, they are all talented, energetic and will further move things forward for sure."

**How the approach to diversity and inclusion has changed and what challenges still exist:**

The challenges facing Diversity and inclusion vary across the legal sector. Simon Colvin has spent over twenty years working at Pinsent Masons and shares his thoughts on what has changed as well as what still needs to change:

"Things have changed amazingly. So, when I joined the firm twenty-one years ago, we did not have an LBGT group and we did not have diversity groups at all. Quite some years ago a few people in the firm got together and said well we do some good stuff and we should give it more focus across the business. That is when the LGBT group was set up and we started to think there are all sorts of other areas of diversity in our firm that are not being given enough focus yet. We then launched Project Sky which is focussed on equality for women at Pinsent Masons and we launched Project Sun which is aimed at promoting race and ethnicity at Pinsent Masons. So now people are investing a lot of time in them because they matter and it has made the firm a better and more well-rounded place to work. We still have a way to go without a doubt it is an ongoing process.

In terms of what needs to change, the legal industry was a traditional profession. It is always going to take a long time to reposition it. It is getting rid of some of those legacy views which are so archaic and outdated. One of the areas is lack of social mobility. Which is why we need to approach how we look into the talent market in a different way so that we enable people who have had more challenges to be able to arrive at the point of consideration for Pinsent Masons and any other law firm. For example, considering applicants regardless of what school or university they attended (and in fact taking that into account for the socially disadvantaged) or what their ethnic background or sexual orientation is - I think that is still a challenge for us as a legal profession."

In addition to these comments, Donya Fredj, Corporate Lawyer, shares her background and what has changed:

"I am a British-Tunisian Muslim female. My mother brought me up single-handedly on a council estate in a deprived area of Norfolk where I attended a state-funded high school and was eligible for free school meals. Watching my mother struggle financially ultimately motivated me to work harder and made me more resilient. Firms that appeal to me are those that believe in the importance of creating a positive and collaborative working environment. As lawyers, it is no secret that we have to work long hours sometimes. Working with people who are approachable and easy to work with makes a huge difference.

Given my multicultural background and experience of upward social mobility, I also look for firms that are committed to enhancing social mobility and embracing diversity and inclusion in the workplace. In my experience, firms that foster an inclusive culture tend to offer a more enriching experience with more opportunity for personal and professional growth.

I attended a high school that, although had some amazing teachers, was known for being a troubled school. My biggest challenge was ignoring the distractions around me and maintaining an optimistic mindset when so many of my peers were losing hope as a result of their circumstances. In order to remain positive, I would look for inspiration wherever I went and constantly remind myself of all the successful people in life who had come from nothing. After literally watching Sister Act 2 about twelve times, my mantra in life became 'If you want to be somebody. If you want to go somewhere. You better wake up and pay attention.' It was my laser-focused determination that led me to achieve my goal at the time of attending the University of Cambridge.

There is a growing focus in the legal industry on diversity and inclusion, with a number of firms offering diversity programmes and initiatives. This must continue in order to widen access to the legal profession. There are many young people who are keen to pursue law but are afraid they will not succeed or fit in because they identify with a group that is under-represented in the legal profession. Mentoring schemes that actively seek to address the under-representation of minority groups are incredibly valuable and I encourage students and young lawyers to actively seek out a mentor who can support them in their career path."

# Chapter 7: Advice for Aspiring Lawyers

This next section aims to provide advice to aspiring lawyers from legal professionals who have experienced different stages of their career and reflect on what they wish they had been told. Over to them for their insight!

**Umar Jamil, Paralegal at Hogan Lovells and Future Trainee Solicitor at Macfarlanes:**

"Take every opportunity to engage with firms - whether it be through law fairs, open days or social platforms, networking with the firm can really help to build an understanding of the firm and what it is like to work there.

Tailor your applications – identify early on which firms you are interested in, and ask yourself why? For example, this may be because of a firm's strength in a specific practice area, diversity and CSR initiatives, small intake or secondment opportunities.

Remember that rejection builds resilience - do not be deterred by rejection, rather use it as an opportunity to reflect and build upon in the next application. Remember that when you do get the offer of a training contract, all your hard work will be worth it and you will become a better trainee solicitor as a result of the obstacles you have had to overcome."

**Benjamin Roach, Associate at Pinsent Masons:**

"For aspiring solicitors, I have two tips. One is do not be disheartened if you do not get a vacation placement or a training contract after your first or second round of applications - and do not give up! For example, I was unsuccessful while applying at university, but I knew it was still what I wanted to do. So, I thought about what else I could do to make myself more employable and develop my skills. If you are unsuccessful, I would suggest looking at other roles like I did such as paralegal roles. And not necessarily at law firms - you could also consider working at companies like I did with the BBC to develop you as a person and get you ready for the next round of applications.

My biggest tip on applications, and maybe it is obvious but it was not to me at first, is to concentrate on quality over quantity. I think in my first year of applying I submitted about thirty-five vacation scheme applications, and that is far too many to maintain the level of quality required. I look back at them now and they are not tailored enough to the particular firm, and when you are up against hundreds of people for the same job, the simple things like that really stand out. I think in the year that I was successful at obtaining my training contract, I did about three applications spending thirty to thirty-five hours on each to do it properly research wise, and interrogate them fully. This approach was far more successful than when I did thirty-five applications, spending about two hours each on.

If I could give myself one piece of advice it would be to be open minded with seat choices. Do not think that not getting a seat the first or second time of trying means 'game over'. It can be quite competitive. Think about what you can learn in those seats to make you a better, more employable lawyer. For instance, I knew that I wanted to do TMT so I picked seats that were contract related (property and pensions). Stay open minded and use the opportunities in each of those seats to your advantage to become a better lawyer in the department you ultimately want to qualify into."

**Joanna Middlemass, Paralegal at Addleshaw Goddard and Future Trainee Solicitor at Ashurst:**

"Crack the basics! There was definitely a point during applying for training contracts that I felt like the penny dropped. Ask yourself, do you really know the difference between a motivational, competency and strength-based question? Could you explain what the difference is and what each requires of you?

If you are splitting yourself across lots of extra-curricular activities, do you know why? Do you know what skills you are developing and how they are transferable to the role of a trainee solicitor? Do you know what a trainee solicitor actually does?

It is really important to sit with yourself and consider these questions (and many more) and write your answers down. The answers will come in useful when drafting applications and preparing for interviews. There are a limited number of motivational, competency and strength-based questions you can be asked. This means you can prepare for every question.

The best piece of advice I was given when I was applying for a training contract was 'it is not a case of if it is a case of when.' This really resonated with me, I felt like I could handle that."

**Vikash Vaitha, Lead Paralegal at Pinsent Masons:**

"Firstly, keep applying to your dream firms if you know they are right for you. Ultimately, only you and the firm will know what is right for you. Secondly, do not be discouraged by rejection. Instead, use this energy to build resilience and drive as these are skills which are necessary for the career. You only need one firm to say yes.

Finally, do not be afraid to express your interests. If you are a musician (like myself), enjoy reading books or have something about you that you really take pride in, do not be afraid to demonstrate your passion for that thing. You will soon realise that your passions have helped you build an amazing personality that should be valued wherever you decide to take it."

**Amelia Wilson, Trainee Solicitor at Channel 4:**

"I would say do not give up! I lacked the confidence that I would be good enough to be a lawyer and it took me a long time to believe in my own abilities, which I still struggle with from time to time. I went to a comprehensive school and did not take a traditional route into law, but I also recognise that being a good lawyer is not just about academics.

I realised that one of my biggest assets is my personal skills. I am a good communicator and work well with people and that has been a great skill to have in television. There are times you need to have difficult conversations with a producer or a sales client, and I find that if they feel you are working collaboratively to find a solution as opposed to just saying 'no you cannot do that' it leads to a far better working relationship.

I would also say work with your talents and try not to compare yourself to others, your own experiences and abilities will make you a different lawyer to the one sitting next to you- that is not a bad thing, our clients are not identical so we should not be."

**Conrad Flaczyk, Knowledge Lawyer at Norton Rose Fulbright:**

i. "Focus on grades/find summaries before law school:

In Canada - and presumably in most jurisdictions - obtaining good grades in law school is the single most productive thing you can do to help secure opportunities in the early stages of your career. It is certainly not the only thing you can do, but good grades go a long way. So, what can you do to obtain good grades in law school? In my experience, the first year of law school is particularly challenging since there are so many new concepts thrown at you, making it difficult to digest and navigate the concepts in the few short months of each term.

It was only towards the end of my first year that I learned that most law schools, whether formally through the law school or informally via Facebook, circulate 'summaries' of past courses, cases, and concepts. At my law school, summaries were often quite comprehensive and accurate. If you are planning for the start of law school or the start of a new semester, consider—prior to the start of the semester—locating a handful of summaries for the class and studying those summaries as if you were preparing for an exam.

Read them carefully, actively, and consider jotting down questions or flagging concepts that are unclear. In this way, when the semester begins, you will have already grasped the basic concepts that other students will be grappling with, and can focus on the more difficult concepts, 'putting it all together', and trying your hand at a few practice exams throughout the semester.

ii. Focus on passing your licensing exams, not applying for jobs:

Understandably so, upper-year law students devote a tremendous amount of time to applying for jobs and networking. As they should. Sometimes, though - after speaking with law students - I find that they can be so ambitious at times that they split their time applying and networking with studying for key licensing exams or accreditation exams (i.e. NCA exams in Canada). While applying and networking are certainly important, passing your licensing exams on the first attempt is likely more important in that instance (as licensing exams are often a few months spread out and failing anyone could delay your licensing date by several months).

Moreover, passing your exams and getting your license will likely make you more attractive to employers who do not run the risk of hiring you and then having to delay your start date. If possible, approach your licensing seriously and aim to pass them on your first shot.

After you do, you can devote 100% of your time and energy on applying for jobs, networking, and building your profile.

iii. Networking is important, but so is building your profile:

While networking and connections may occasionally lead to jobs in the early stages of a legal career—in my opinion—this is the rare exception and not the rule. Focusing on your candidate profile and application letters is likely more productive if you wish to find work at a large or mid-sized law firm. And here is why. Large law firms receive hundreds of applications for entry level positions, which means they must have certain bureaucratic processes and procedures in place for handling those applications.

This often means they have HR and Talent teams with over twenty people, and, before any decision is made on an application, there is a good chance that five to ten people read your application. In that circumstance, even if you have a strong connection with any one lawyer or HR manager, it is unlikely that any one person on the hiring committee has enough influence to propose hiring a candidate whose application or profile was not near the top of the pile. And, even if your connection had such influence, they would have to put their professional reputation on the line to vouch for your profile (which would be risky if your application was not competitive with stronger candidates).

Finally, most lawyers at large to mid-sized firms are entirely removed from the hiring process (as they are not members of the hiring committee). As a result, spending time to network with such lawyers with the sole intention of finding work can be counterproductive, unless that time is spent learning about the firm and making your application letters targeted and competitive.

For all of these reasons, I often stress the importance of spending your time building a strong profile or application, such as: good grades, gaining business or other professional experience, publishing, getting involved in the community, or trying something bold like starting a venture, charity, awareness campaign, blog, podcast, or other initiative.

But, whatever you do, make sure to produce some tangible results that you can later market in your application documents and that will make you stand out as a candidate.

iv. Under promise but over deliver:

As a summer student or junior lawyer, you will be assigned work randomly by different lawyers at the firm (none of which know what other lawyers have assigned you). This means that you have to be very careful in accepting work and setting deadlines, as most are eager to accept everything that comes their way. I found that a handy trick for preventing any issues is to 'under promise but over deliver'.

When being assigned work, try negotiating a deadline that is as far back as possible, but then delivering early. Having more time is always better because, in law firms, you can randomly be assigned something 'urgent' that needs priority, so, if you promise to deliver 'by the end of the day', you might get a new assignment following your meeting that needs to be done immediately and this can cause trouble.

For that same reason, when you get assigned work, try to start immediately (even if promised to deliver in a week) as you have no idea what will be assigned tomorrow. If you simply do the work you are assigned, meet your deadlines, and do a reasonably good job, you will almost certainly impress as a student.

v.      Do not give way to imposter syndrome. You were hired for a reason:

To be a lawyer, you had to study hard, be admitted to law school, and pass your licensing exams. None of those were easy, and each is a big achievement in and of itself. So, once you are hired and secure a training contract, give yourself the benefit of the doubt. You were hired for a reason. While you are young, you are also smart and eager to learn. Junior lawyers often feel that they do not know enough - or have imposter syndrome. But, in order to truly thrive in the legal profession, it is important to overcome that feeling. Of course, you must be cautious in the advice you give - making sure you are giving competent advice - but do not be afraid to put yourself out there or take on work you might not be familiar with to learn new skills. It is a profession where the amount you put in is the amount you get out."

**Daniel Lo, Legal Counsel at UBS:**

"Start to work on your personal branding early. I know not many lawyers think that this is an area they should be concerned with, but the practice of law is as much about law as it is relationships.

Developing your personal brand will allow you to build more relationships, with the hope that some of these relationships will either translate into clients later on when you are trying to build a book of business or become your knowledge referral network."

**Deepti Patankar, Ex-Associate at Linklaters:**

"For trainee solicitors and aspiring solicitors, spend time reading up precedent and know how notes. This will put you ahead in your work. As a trainee solicitor whenever you are given a task, be mindful of the context, ask questions so that you learn more and go read up more so that you know how things work rather than just doing the task for the sake of it.

Your best progress tracker is your principal and associate buddies. You should invest in relationships with mid-level associates who you can use as sounding boards!"

**Jade Naylor, Trainee Solicitor at Pinsent Masons:**

"Having pursued the paralegal route, I have the following tips and advice for aspiring solicitors. Do not give up because you will have setbacks, but you need to be resilient and determined in order to secure a training contract. Take your time with the applications and do your research; I worked full time in the week as a paralegal and so I spent a fair few weekends over the summer of 2017 dedicating all my time to applying, which was not the most enjoyable especially as it was so warm outside but it is that kind of determination that will in the end make you succeed."

**Jennifer O'Kane, Trainee Solicitor at Simmons & Simmons:**

"Reach out to trainee solicitors. Associates and the graduate recruitment team at the firm and ask lots of questions. This will help you better understand the culture of the firm you are applying for and if it is somewhere you could envisage yourself working. It is also great to attend as many events at different firms as possible - this will help when you are interviewing as all the faces will be more familiar and the process will seem less daunting."

**Laura Durrant, Director of Howlett Brown Limited:**

"If I could turn it around and say what is the worst piece of advice I have received, I would say that it is that I should not look above my station and that I should moderate my ambitions. Young people should be encouraged to shoot for the stars, with advice focused on what they need to do to achieve it. But unfortunately, some people feel the need to reinforce their own limitations by sharing them with others.

Be flexible and open to opportunities and make sure you are always making a choice to be somewhere. Careers are long and need to be challenging and fun. Some people find that their first job allows for progression and that one organisation has everything that they need and that is great. Others move several times and that is great too. Just make sure you are actively managing your career, picking up skills as you go, and always choosing where to be, even if it is exactly where you started."

**Louise Formisano, Trainee Solicitor at CMS:**

"Whilst it might be patronising to say this, given I have had a very traditional path into the career (university, LPC, training contract), I want to stress that you should not feel compelled to follow this cookie-cutter approach. The average age to qualify as a solicitor in the UK is twenty-nine, and I am surrounded by people in my cohort who have had varied and enriched experiences before starting their training contracts, which I am envious of. I wish I knew that it is okay not to have secured a training contract in second or third year - it is actually normal!

If you are rejected this time round, it is just another opportunity to take the year ahead of you as time to better yourself even more so that your next application showcases a completely new, reformed and enhanced version of the last version of you that applied."

**Matthew Wilson, Associate General Counsel, EMEA & APAC at Uber:**

"Be yourself. Be authentic. Be curious. Have confidence. Have courage. I have always thought that when you go for interviews and you are looking at training contracts, or thinking about qualification and you are going for those jobs in certain departments the attitude you need to have is that someone needs to get these jobs and the jobs are available because they need to be filled. Companies need to fill those spots so it might as well be you that fills them! If you have that attitude then you can go into those sessions with humility but also with confidence, believing in yourself. That gets you a long way.

In all organisations there is an increasing recognition around the world that diversity and inclusion have a lot of power. Typically, we think of diversity as colour, ethnicity, wealth, gender and so on, and diversity comes in all shapes and sizes. It can be all those things but it can also be diversity of qualifications, diversity of background or diversity of age. In our teams we try and put together all different kinds of diversity. Whatever your background or education might be - all of that adds to the diversity mix as opposed to building teams where everyone has the same qualifications and backgrounds.

There are unifying characteristics you want in any person you bring into a team, like being a decent, friendly human being, as you want a new person to work and integrate with the team easily and ensure that they are not going to destroy the cohesiveness or well-being of the team! By having diverse teams, it raises the bar and raises the expectation of everybody to be more curious, more thoughtful and less lazy. That is because by having different perspectives it means the team is more likely to get different options on the table and pick the best one. Which is why it is so important to include diversity and diverse opinions in all the conversations you have when decision making."

**Niall McCluskey Advocate at Optimum Advocates based in Glasgow:**

"Get involved in groups such as law societies, citizen's advice bureau and student law centres. Most importantly of all, build a network in the profession. From an early stage contact legal organisations, solicitors, advocates and barristers and try and get as much work experience or shadowing as possible. Traineeships often come out of these connections.

Big firms and organisations tend to have very formal processes for recruiting and tend to interview very early in the degree process so make sure you familiarise yourself with what is expected if you want these types of jobs. Smaller firms tend to recruit much later on.

If you want to do court work then engage in public speaking and mooting. Become very computer literate. Increasingly advocacy will be remote so good computer skills are essential. Furthermore, almost all documents are transmitted electronically now so being able to organise material without hard copies is a great skill to have."

**Sajeed Jamal, Trainee Solicitor at Trowers & Hamlins:**

"If you can, find a 'mentor' - someone to proofread, give you honest feedback and help you stay positive and put set-backs into perspective. This person does not necessarily need to be in the legal profession. But most of all just preserve and be unreasonably positive.

My advice is to keep on slogging away and focus on yourself. The world is full of people showing you the highlights reel but what you do not see is the hours of sheer grit, determination and handwork to manifest those achievements.

As an aspiring lawyer - try to learn and develop every single day. Focus on being better than the last day. You need to have a blinkered approach. Life is not easy, and everything takes hard work and graft, doors will not suddenly open. You have to knock and keep knocking until they do. My main advice is just to keep preserving. When that training contract offer comes, and it will, it will be all worth it.

Also, I only focussed my applications on around six firms, that is why you can spend so much time on each application and get them perfected, reviewed and edited before submitting. You can also review what they are doing in the marketplace, read about the latest deals they have advised on and know what their long-vision is. You cannot do this with fifty law firms!

I say this because the main hurdle with applications is bypassing the application stage where there are thousands of applicants. This way your applications are tailored and will really stand out from the hundreds of others in that pile."

## Scott Halliday, Associate at Irwin Mitchell:

"I would really encourage candidates for whatever firm/chambers and in whatever practice area to remember the importance of being authentic. It is essential to feel able to be yourself in your workplace and this is especially true of candidates from a diverse background. My advice is to do your research on firms in terms of culture and personnel on the ground and trust your instinct. There are firms who are really trying to address diversity and inclusion. I urge you to gravitate to those firms. The only other advice I would give is cliché, but it is essential and that is work hard, work really very hard. To be a lawyer is an absolute privilege, deliver great client service and be the very best you can be."

## Simon Colvin, Global Head of Technology at Pinsent Masons:

"Read as much as you can around where your focus and passion are. No matter which firm you are looking at or if you are looking for an in-house role the most important piece of advice I could give is to develop your understanding of what that the ideal role looks like so that A –

you are best informed to know where is the best fit for you and B – that when you engage and start out your career you can be as compelling and successful as possible.

We live in a competitive world and demonstrating that you have really gone the extra mile is important. I think innovation and doing things that shows you have thought outside the box is important instead of following the traditional path are always going to get you further because it demonstrates so many good qualities.

Everyone has a different area that they are really stimulated by and I think the most important thing is that you do what really appeals to you. For example, on the question of would you be a litigator or a transactional lawyer, most people will have an immediate view. Once you have got that view and recognise what feels like a natural transition for you then you should stick with it. If you have got the passion for that area and are willing to go the extra mile then you are more likely to succeed."

**Vaibhav Adlakha, Associate at Reed Smith:**

"To any aspiring lawyers with a disability who believes there are barriers or limitations entering the legal sector I would say to know what your ability is rather than what disability you have. Know how you are going to work within the profession and how your disability will affect the environment, you want to be in.

For example, in the beginning I thought I could be a good transactional lawyer but soon found out that the pace of transactional work was not for me. Therefore, one needs to understand what expectations the clients may have and how can you fulfil those expectations. At the end of the day, you want to be treated the same as everyone else and have the same expectations from clients and colleagues.

Which is why it is important to know how your disability works and how you are able to do the work that is expected of you with the limitations that you have, this is the key to entering the profession. The journey from disability to ability is a tough one so be sure to have a good support network around you as they will advise you further on what the best environment might be for you."

**Lukas Vivian, Trainee Solicitor at CMS:**

"Do not wait for the last moment to apply and do not apply to any law firm just because it is open for applications. It cannot be a matter of quantity above quality. I remember that I was applying to over twenty law firms for their vacation schemes and/or directly for their training contracts. It was however only three law firms where I invested time and it was these three with whom I got an initial interview. If I could go back in time, I would focus and really take my time to properly convey my interest to only the three that were top of my list.

Additionally, I found it helpful to attend dinners, drinks or any other social events organised by the university law societies or the firms themselves. I know I missed a few that I wanted to attend, so my advice would be to try and attend as many as possible. Meeting the current trainee solicitors at the law firms can give you so much more than just researching the law firms online or talking to recruiters. If I was applying for training contracts now, I would have found it much easier to answer questions and would be much more confident during the interviews. If you can find trainee solicitors who are happy to discuss their experiences with you, you will be much better off.

My path towards a training contract was a bit different, as it involved studying my Bachelor's degree in law in The Netherlands and an LLM at Cambridge. There are no lawyers in my family and none of my family live in London. It was only in Cambridge when I had a chance to properly research various law firms in London and attend some law fairs that listed the various options for me. I expected that the then upcoming merger between CMS Cameron McKenna, Nabarro and Olswang would create a truly global player that could easily compete with the Magic Circle firms.

I saw a lot of potential in the merger and wanted to be one of the first trainee solicitors experiencing the vacation scheme at a newly merged firm. In addition to that, CMS was one of the largest law firms in Europe, constantly growing, and coming from Slovakia I thought that this might be the best fit for me.

My first piece of advice is therefore to do your homework on the various law firms and not to decide based on superficial reasons such as 'this is a magic circle firm that is known worldwide and all my friends/family would be delighted'. It is much more important for the law firm to fit well with what you expect from life as you will inevitably want to grow.

I did not think my international legal background would be of interest to any of the city law firms as I thought it would be too rigid for their requirements. However, if you really want to achieve something and follow your interests, you will succeed. I can also see the benefits of attending as many vacation schemes as possible, over a few summers while at university. During the course of two-three weeks, the experience will give you an idea as to whether this profession is for you and whether you would be able to commit significant time and energy to become a qualified lawyer.

You just have to start applying early and really put the time into the application process, as it will surely pay off one way or another. Quality is always above quantity. It is your decision and it needs to come from you, no one else."

**Mental Health:**

**Simon Colvin, Global Head of Technology at Pinsent Masons:**

Having worked in the legal sector for over twenty years, Simon Colvin shares his insight on Mental Health and what has changed:

"At Pinsent Masons, the Mindful Business Charter started out as a programme with our clients but of course we were able to say we were practising what we preached. The good thing about Pinsents is that it has always been not only a place of diversity but also a place of very little hierarchy and therefore allowing people to operate in their own way was always going to be something we embraced. That is where the Mindful Business Charter fitted in so well. So, I think it has been really successful and is kind of an extension of how the firm operated anyway but has now been enshrined with some more tangible rules.

I think COVID-19 has kickstarted some early monumental changes in businesses full stop so the question for us will be how does our operating model change in the longer term and what do we want to do about where we work, how we keep our teams motivated and how we keep our junior staff on a strong trajectory from their career's perspective. I think managing that will be a big short-term issue that we think about quite carefully.

Other issues that I have seen raised in the news recently is whether great initiatives relating to diversity and the mindful business are being put on the backburner in light of COVID-19. I think absolutely not. Those things are there for a reason and we stand by them, so it is ensuring that we keep those areas running and with a strong focus. So, without a doubt the next three to five years will be really quite interesting. The firm has moved into a position where it is a professional services firm with the law at its core. So related skills such as project management and technology provision provide a broader service for clients which means we are better equipped to help them.

I think what is great is that the issues around mental health has really been taken out of the closet and people have stood up and said I have had mental health issues. Without a doubt being in a law firm can be challenging at times and it can be demanding and exhausting. I think being able to embrace people when they come to work with whatever situation they find themselves in is really important which is why having champions in the business so that our people can talk more openly is really important. I think now that it is out and we have that message it means no one needs to be worried about hiding those issues and instead they can raise them at the workplace and will receive full support."

**Carolyn Pepper, Partner at Reed Smith and co-chair of the disability inclusion group LEADRS:**

"Reed Smith recently established a Mental Health Task Force, which works to support the firm's policies in this area and to de-stigmatise mental health issues in the legal industry. We also have numerous wellness initiatives and training sessions available.

Mental health is as important as physical health and should be treated no differently.
On the preventative side, the legal industry needs to make sure that people prioritise their mental health and have the time to do so. We also need to recognise the signs of a mental health problem and give people the confidence to ask for help before it becomes overwhelming.

I think people are far more willing to talk about mental health problems now than they were a few years ago. When people recognise that having a mental health difficulty is no barrier to a successful career or promotion, things will begin to change.

Flexibility is key to achieve a good work/life balance. The legal profession is a demanding one but enabling people to work in a way that suits them can make a big difference."

**Donya Fredj, Corporate Lawyer:**

"I think the first step is for the legal profession to fully acknowledge the importance of mental health and work on removing any stigma that is attached to mental health problems by encouraging open dialogue. This will help ensure that those who are struggling with their mental health feel supported and have the courage to ask for help when needed.

There is a perception that lawyers at U.S. firms work longer hours than other lawyers. However, that is not necessarily the case. The reality is that working for any leading law firm in the city will involve long and unpredictable hours at times. The impact of technology has also meant that work now seeps into our daily lives. In order to handle the demands of work effectively, the best thing lawyers can do is to ensure they take care of both their physical and mental health. In particular, I think it is important that lawyers do something that allows them to switch off completely every day even if just for a short period of time. Personally, I love going out for a walk in the fresh air."

# Conclusion

If you have made it this far, thank you all for reading the range of insights shared by our contributors. If you have any questions regarding this publication, feel free to drop me a line directly via my contact details below. Once again, a huge thank you to everyone who gave up their time to make this project happen.

**Matthew Berrick Contact Details:**

LinkedIn: https://www.linkedin.com/in/matthew-berrick-4210ba49/

Email: legallineup@gmail.com

**Additional Free Resources:**

**TC Application Guide (130+ Pages):**

https://drive.google.com/file/d/1Bnq97cJoS-eM8qsS9sO3hEMIpVkJ73HQ/view?usp=sharing

**Interview Tips:**

https://drive.google.com/file/d/18NTNG0HMPPE9GHfcJz4VdA-l7qnEgPO8/view?usp=sharing

Printed in Great Britain
by Amazon